The Politics of
Comprehensive
Manpower Legislation

Roger H. Davidson

The Johns Hopkins University Press, Baltimore and London

The Johns Hopkins University Press, Baltimore, Maryland 21218
The Johns Hopkins University Press Ltd., London

Library of Congress Catalog Card Number: 72–10874
ISBN 0–8018–1471–5 (cloth)
ISBN 0–8018–1470–7 (paper)

Library of Congress Cataloging in Publication Data will be found on the last
printed page of this book.

Contents

Acknowledgments

Many people assisted me in preparing this study, and it would be impossible for me to acknowledge adequately my debts to them. Many administrators, legislators, interest-group representatives and outside observers gave freely of their time to share with me their experiences and insights. In most cases these people were promised anonymity. In a very real sense, this is their book. No outside student of governmental affairs can hope to learn his subject without the cooperation and goodwill of those whose daily responsibilities fall within the subject matter. Therefore, I gladly acknowledge their contribution.

This research was made possible by the National Manpower Policy Task Force, where I served as scholar in residence during the 1970–71 academic year. The task force's Vice Chairman, Sar A. Levitan, has over the years been a constant counselor, guide, and friend. The full measure of my indebtedness to him can never be expressed adequately. Lowell M. Glenn, then executive director of the task force, was able to arrange all the details, both large and small, that made my tenure with the task force enjoyable and profitable. In addition, he offered many useful substantive suggestions. The study was prepared under a contract to the task force from the Office of Research and Development, Manpower Administration, U.S. Department of Labor. Dr. Howard Rosen, director of the Office, gave me the benefit of his vast experience in the manpower field. At the same time, he insisted on permitting me the utmost freedom to pursue my own interests in the manner that I thought best.

In addition to Dr. Levitan, the following persons read and commented upon an earlier version of the manuscript: Dr. Garth L. Mangum of the University of Utah; Dr. Peter Kobrak of the University of Wisconsin-Milwaukee; Ms. Trish Hogue, formerly legislative assistant to Representative William A. Steiger; Jim Harrison, Staff Director of the House Subcommittee on Agricultural Labor; and several officials from the Manpower Administration, U.S. Department of Labor. Their care and patience are greatly appreciated. During the preparation of this study, I was fortunate to have the efficient secretarial assistance of Ms. Penelope Scarburgh and Ms. Ivis Steele.

Needless to add, I assume full responsibility for the facts and conclusions reported here.

Santa Barbara, California

The Politics of Comprehensive Manpower Legislation

1
Manpower Programs Come of Age

The word "manpower" is a fairly new addition to the lexicon, but we have always had manpower policies in the largest sense—policies affecting the size, skills, and disposition of the working force. Indeed, one of the problems of defining manpower programs is their ubiquity; immigration, slavery, land laws, and universal education were all at their heart manpower policies, and today the most potent manpower decisions are those made in defense spending, selective service, research and technology, and a host of other decisions that affect where government's resources are directed.[1] In recent years, however, explicit concern over manpower policies has focused upon remedial programs—training and services for those who need help in finding a job, developing adequate skills, and otherwise adjusting to the world of work. Some programs focus upon the supply side of the labor market, preparing the disadvantaged for gainful employment; others are directed to the demand side, opening doors for disadvantaged workers in the private sector. Finally, some programs simply seek to improve the functioning of the labor market, matching up

[1] Garth L. Mangum, *The Emergence of Manpower Policy* (New York: Holt, Rinehart & Winston, 1969), pp. 12 ff.

1

supply and demand more effectively and setting standards and minimums for low-income employment.[2]

Concerted federal efforts to alleviate joblessness and impoverishment date primarily from the New Deal period. Among the more enduring innovations were creation of the federal-state employment security system, establishment of state public welfare agencies, and legal standing for labor unions to bargain for workers. Of equal or greater importance, the New Deal's legacy embraced a growing commitment on the government's part to act directly and explicitly to foster economic well-being. Philosophically, the culminating statement of this commitment was found in the Employment Act of 1946, which spoke of "the continuing policy and responsibility of the federal government . . . to foster and promote . . . maximum employment, production, and purchasing power."[3]

The Employment Act's promise was not immediately fulfilled; but the "second New Deal" of the 1960s produced a host of new manpower programs designed to help people prepare for, and adjust to, the world of work. In 1961, federally sponsored manpower efforts consisted mainly of vocational education and rehabilitation, the federal-state employment service, an apprenticeship program, and a program for importing low-cost farm labor in harvest seasons. Total cost of the programs did not exceed $250 million. By the end of the decade, expenditures approached $4 billion annually for a wide variety of programs, including numerous training and work-experience opportunities, an enlarged employment service, and a program designed to move people from welfare into productive employment. Many of these programs were attached to two major pieces of legislation: the Manpower Development and Training Act (MDTA) of 1962, and the Economic Opportunity Act of 1964. In short, the decade saw meaning

[2] See Sar A. Levitan, *Programs in Aid of the Poor for the 1970s* (Baltimore: The Johns Hopkins Press, 1969).

[3] A discussion of the philosophical foundations of the Employment Act is found in Stephen K. Bailey's fascinating history, *Congress Makes a Law* (New York: Columbia University Press, 1950), chap. 2.

given to the Employment Act's commitment and elevation of manpower considerations to what Garth Mangum calls "key independent status" in policymaking.[4]

COMPETING AGENCIES AND THEIR CLIENTELES

In the competition to gain control over these burgeoning programs, the Department of Labor possessed important resources. Since the New Deal period, the department has embraced the largest employment agency in the nation, the U.S. Employment Service (now the Training and Employment Service), whose 50 state employment security agencies and their 2,200 local offices are potentially capable of providing more basic manpower services than any other single organization. Wholly subsidized by the federal government, the system is nonetheless state run and locally oriented. By serving several masters, the employment services have often ended by serving none. Many efforts have been made to wield more vigorous federal control over the system, especially to harness its resources to serve disadvantaged and poverty-stricken workers. Internal reorganization in 1969 brought this objective closer to reality.[5]

Before 1962 the Labor Department's activities—aside from the employment service—were confined largely to generating labor statistics and handling labor disputes. In that year, however, MDTA launched a modest training program for unemployed but experienced adult workers. The manpower act was originally viewed as a way of protecting laborers against the effects of automation; but as the decade progressed and general employment soared, MDTA was broadened by a series of amendments to encompass a variety of objectives and services.[6] The emphasis shifted

[4] Mangum, *The Emergence of Manpower Policy*, pp. 160–61. See also Stanley H. Ruttenberg (assisted by Jocelyn Gutchess), *Manpower Challenge of the 1970s: Institutions and Social Change* (Baltimore: The Johns Hopkins Press, 1970), pp. 3–4.

[5] See Ruttenberg, pp. 77 ff.

[6] These changes are detailed in Garth L. Mangum, *MDTA: Foundation of Federal Manpower Policy* (Baltimore: The Johns Hopkins Press, 1968).

3

toward workers who suffered severe handicaps in competing for available jobs—unemployed youths, low-skilled workers, minority groups, and the elderly. MDTA has continued to enjoy bipartisan support: liberals favor training programs because they increase total federal expenditures and thus help stimulate aggregate demand, while conservatives view them as devices to aid the free market in bringing together qualified laborers and jobs.

A second manpower agency is the Department of Health, Education, and Welfare, whose Office of Education administers the vocational education program. Begun on a national scale in 1917, "voc ed" is a grant-in-aid program to the 50 state education agencies, which in turn channel the money to local school systems to conduct training programs, either as part of the regular secondary school curriculum or in special adult programs. Traditionally, the federal government has exercised few restraints on how the money is spent, and curriculum and techniques have been slow to respond to altered needs. Even into the 1960s, agriculture and home economics dominated the curriculum. The sprawling conglomerate that is HEW has tended to treat vocational education as a poor cousin, in part because the Office of Education has been led by officials biased in favor of general education.

A third major competitor for manpower programs was the Office of Economic Opportunity (OEO). The Economic Opportunity Act of 1964 was largely a package of manpower programs aimed at providing jobs or preparing the employable poor for jobs. During the early years of the act, OEO tended to be staffed by people unfamiliar with the federal bureaucracy. Thus the agency was often clumsy in jockeying for position. The scandal-prone nature of some of the antipoverty programs, coupled with frequent loose administration, further gave the agency a bad name around Washington.[7] Antipoverty programs have therefore been gradually "spun off" to old-line agencies, mainly the Department of Labor.

[7] The most comprehensive evaluation of the "war on poverty" is Sar A. Levitan's *The Great Society's Poor Law* (Baltimore: The Johns Hopkins Press, 1969).

4

The antipoverty programs reversed the usual procedure of channeling manpower services through state governments; indeed, they often bypassed local governments as well. The most controversial part of the legislation was an open-ended program of federal grants to local community action agencies (CAA's)—organizations designed to stimulate and coordinate a variety of social welfare services for the poor. Local community action programs were to be "developed, conducted, and administered with the maximum feasible participation of residents of the areas and members of the group served." The local CAA's proved to be lightning rods for conflict. Unlike traditional agencies, the CAA's were run by people who were from or otherwise close to disadvantaged and minority populations. Of the more than 1,000 CAA's which sprung up, most were—and continue to be—nonprofit, nongovernmental organizations. In some spectacular instances, they brought down the wrath of officials in state houses and city halls. Hostile politicians, not to mention critical observers like Daniel Patrick Moynihan, seized upon these incidents as evidence that the antipoverty programs were ill conceived or pernicious, or both;[8] but as time passed the hostilities dwindled and have virtually disappeared. Indeed, the vast majority of CAA's served simply as an administrative vehicle for work which community agencies had already been doing; and the bulk of the funds undoubtedly found their way back to such established institutions as schools, welfare agencies, and local charities.

THE STRUGGLE FOR ADMINISTRATIVE COORDINATION

Coordination among the major federal agencies competing for preeminence in the manpower field was frequently discussed in the 1960s, but little was accomplished. However, the period saw the Labor Department, led by a succession of vigorous administrators, strengthen its hold on federal manpower programs, taking over old programs and gaining assignment of new ones. HEW's passivity

[8] Daniel Patrick Moynihan, *Maximum Feasible Misunderstanding* (New York: The Free Press, 1969).

5

and OEO's impotence aided the Department of Labor's expansion.

As early as 1964, a President's Commission on Manpower was created to bring agency heads together and advise the president; but Labor Secretary Willard Wirtz, the chairman, would not permit the group to discuss fundamental problems for fear of spreading his department's jurisdiction to others. Later the commission sent three-man task forces (representing the Labor Department, HEW, and OEO) to explore problems and try to integrate local manpower efforts in thirty localities. Not surprisingly, the task forces found that coordination was desperately needed; but after some limited successes, their efforts were curtailed.[9] Another attempt at coordination, the Concentrated Employment Program (CEP), dating from 1967, was an effort by Secretary Wirtz to extend his department's influence by targeting slum area manpower efforts under strong direction from the Manpower Administration. From the beginning CEP was plagued by jurisdictional conflicts between OEO and Labor, ending in a treaty signed by the two agencies whereby the local CAA's were to be the program sponsors in each CEP area, while the employment service would be the "presumptive provider of manpower services." The arrangement did nothing to reduce conflict between the rival agencies and led to mind-boggling administrative complexities. A congressional mandate for coordination, embodied in the 1967 Economic Opportunity Act amendments, went unheeded because OEO and Labor could not get together on language for a delegation agreement to slice up the pie.

Such rivalry among federal agencies was bound to be reflected in the states and localities, where the manpower dollars eventually went. As James Fesler has written, ". . . Field problems are less *sui generis* than a mirroring of problems at the center."[10] A hierarchy of local and state interagency committees, called CAMPS (Cooperative Area Manpower Planning System), was introduced administratively in 1967 to provide more consistent planning for

[9] Mangum, *MDTA*, pp. 136 ff.; Ruttenberg, pp. 30 ff.
[10] James Fesler, *Area and Administration* (University, Ala.: University of Alabama Press, 1949), p. 74.

manpower programs.[11] At the bottom of the structure are some 400 local CAMPS committees, which are supposed to assess their area's needs for manpower services, balance these against available resources, determine priorities, and coordinate local efforts to deal with the priorities. Local plans are passed on to state and then regional committees, which combine the documents into larger ones. The CAMPS committees brought together people from disparate agencies, but the resultant "plans" were only compilations of individual program requests. Labor Secretary George Shultz observed that the unity in the documents was often limited to the use of a common staple to hold the individual plans together. Because CAMPS committees had no authority over allocating funds, their discussions were little more than academic exercises. Individual agencies were "glad to use the CAMPS to find out what the others are doing, but they do not regard CAMPS as the arena within which to fight for the prize."

Program fragmentation is a product not only of agency rivalries but also, and more fundamentally, of the manner in which policies are formulated and sustained in a pluralist political system. As each new pressing need is identified and publicized, a remedy or palliative is fashioned in the form of a governmental program. Thus governmental involvement tends to be a mosaic of single-purpose efforts, with inevitable discord.

Once a program is launched, its authors, implementors, and clients comprise a lobby dedicated to perpetuating the activity. Older programs boast well-established professional organizations—in vocational education, the American Vocational Association; in the employment service, the Interstate Conference of Employment Security Agencies (ICESA), which is actually staffed and housed in the Labor Department. Many of the new programs generated in the 1960s soon generated their own supportive groups. For example, local poverty workers are represented by the National

---

[11] The CAMPS operation is described in Ruttenberg, pp. 47–51; Mangum, *MDTA*, pp. 73–75; and Howard Hallman *et al., State Manpower Organization* (Washington, D.C.: Center for Governmental Studies, July 1970), pp. 21–24.

Association for Community Development (NACD, or "Naked," as it is called). Single-purpose programs often garner additional support from large multipurpose lobbying groups who benefit from the services in some way. Manpower policies are closely followed by a number of such groups, including the AFL-CIO, the U.S. Chamber of Commerce, the U.S. Conference of Mayors–League of Cities, the Leadership Conference on Civil Rights, and Common Cause. Interest groups insist that programs and funds be earmarked for the purposes they desire and resist attempts to emasculate or combine programs.

Such a piecemeal approach is natural enough, but in the aggregate the federal edifice has reached gingerbread proportions. Annual funding is provided program by program, since congressional appropriations committees (not to mention outside clientele groups) stoutly resist lump-sum or program budgeting. Once appropriated, the funds may go from the federal agency to the states (as in vocational education, the employment security system, and much of MDTA) or to the localities (as in CEP and most of the antipoverty programs). Some programs are funded by formulas designed to reward those localities where a problem—unemployment, crop disease, or whatever—is concentrated; but such formulas are no more than rough approximations of need. Other programs proceed by letting contracts: federal bureaucrats hang up their sign, and local contractors come running to compete for money. This often results in a game of governmental grantsmanship, in which money tends to flow into localities (especially large cities) blessed with talented staff people who are experienced in writing up federal grant applications. In other words, the rich areas get richer while the poor get poorer.

People needing manpower services find these arrangements frustrating and sometimes dehumanizing. Each individual program represents a different hoop through which would-be recipients must jump to receive help. Surrounding each program is a plethora of application forms, guidelines, and reporting procedures. Such complexities are not entirely the products of a bureaucratic mentality; in altogether too many instances, bureaucrats simply adopt arcane

8

procedures to discourage applications when Congress has not provided enough money to go around. On the other hand, duplication of services is rife; adult basic education, for example, is available from eleven different grant programs, prevocational and skill training from ten, and on-the-job training from five. Local program sponsors and potential clients frequently find it hard to fit their unique needs into governmental program definitions.

Frustration at these patterns of arrangements mounted in the 1960s, as scores of new special-purpose programs were piled on top of basic service institutions dating from the New Deal or before. Such troubles are by no means limited to the manpower field but extend to virtually every type of domestic governmental activity. The dilemma is epitomised by a true story from the mid-1960s. It seems that the mayor of a small Wisconsin town was trying to obtain money for an antipoverty program. After studying the forbidding packet of instructions and application forms, he discovered that neither he, his lawyer, nor his United States senator could figure them out. Finally, he told his senator that it would be simpler and more efficient if then-OEO Director Sargent Shriver would simply charter a plane from Chicago, fly over the little town, and dump the money out so the town fathers could spend it as they saw fit. When informed of the mayor's desperation, Shriver replied that he couldn't comply—the law did not authorize him to charter a plane![12]

Bringing order out of such chaos will obviously require more than chartering planes to dump money around the country. The frustrating history of comprehensive manpower legislation between 1969 and 1971 is instructive not only because it reveals the inner workings of manpower policymaking but also because it illustrates how difficult it is to make repairs in the structure of administrative and political pluralism which has been erected.

---

[12] Related in U.S. Senate, Committee on Labor and Public Welfare, Subcommittee on Employment, Manpower, and Poverty, *Manpower Development and Training Legislation, 1970*, 91st Cong., 1st and 2nd sess. (Washington, D.C., 1970), pt. 1, p. 154.

2

Legislative Approaches to Reform

As attested by the frequent though fruitless attempts at coordination, the growing confusion within the manpower subgovernment did not escape notice. People who were in a position to take an overview of what was happening—top-level administrators, outside academic observers, and a few knowledgeable legislators—were the first to call for changes in delivery mechanisms. Gradually there developed within the higher levels of the Manpower Administration a set of what one insider called "mostly intuitive precepts" concerning the desirable direction of change. The development of these precepts can be traced in major policy documents and guidelines developed internally by the Labor Department in 1967–68, as such programs as CEP and CAMPS were set in motion and then assessed. Perhaps the most influential statement of the emerging ideas about decentralizing delivery systems was a seminar paper on the states' manpower role, prepared for the National Governors' Conference in 1968 by University of Utah manpower expert Garth L. Mangum. The proposals embodied in Mangum's paper found their way into two significant task force reports and at least one legislative proposal.[1] The evolution of

[1] Garth L. Mangum, "The Governor's Role in Federal Manpower Programs for the Disadvantaged" (Paper prepared for the Executive Committee and Manpower and Labor Relations Committee of the National Governors' Conference, 1968).

ideas proceeded with the bipartisanship typical of manpower programs in the 1960s—receiving eager support from two successive secretaries of labor, Willard Wirtz and George Shultz, and leadership from their assistant secretaries for manpower, Stanley Ruttenberg and Arnold Weber.

The consensus view concerning manpower reform was epitomised in the report of President-elect Nixon's Task Force on Manpower and Labor-Management Decisions, one of ten such task forces appointed following the 1968 election to study domestic problems and submit reports for the new administration. Chairman of the group was Shultz, who was later named as Nixon's first secretary of labor. In its December 1968 report, the Shultz task force identified four key problems in manpower programs: (1) the backlog of unemployed and underemployed people had required remedial efforts to the neglect of preventive ones; (2) the *ad hoc* legislative approach had produced overlapping programs; (3) national programs created by federal initiative were not flexible enough to meet local situations; and (4) the program approach confined clients within program requirements rather than conforming services to individual needs.

The Shultz task force concluded that a comprehensive manpower act was badly needed for "consolidating the lessons of experience into a single manageable program offering services adapted to community and individual need." The legislation would authorize a full range of available services without fixing the proportion of available funds to be allocated among the functions. This implied consolidating all remedial manpower programs within one federal agency, presumably the Department of Labor. Along with consolidation, the task force came down strongly for decentralization of decisionmaking.

While the federal agency should maintain a strong presence by issuing guidelines, approving or disapproving plans and proposals, evaluating performance and providing technical assistance, the actual delivery of services, except in rare circumstances, should be the responsibility of units of state and local governments.

11

State or local governments, it was reasoned, would be responsive to clientele groups through the ballot box and constituency pressure. Funds would be allocated to the states by formula, with a "pass-through" requirement to assure that funds reached the major cities. A portion of the funds would remain with the federal government for interstate programs, research, experimentation, technical assistance, and "service to populations neglected by recalcitrant states." For the individual client, the objective was one which had been urged by manpower experts from the beginning: a single contact point at the community level where the client could gain access to available manpower services.

At the same time the National Manpower Policy Task Force— an organization of academic manpower experts funded by the Manpower Administration to promote manpower policy research— expressed similar conclusions in their first position paper.[2] Summarizing the experience of the 1960s, the group urged a streamlined, comprehensive manpower enactment in which manpower services would be grouped along functional rather than program lines and allocated according to community and individual needs. A single legislative package and a single appropriations process would be required; a unified federal manpower agency would also be desirable, though not necessary. Whatever the organizational mechanism, ". . . administrators should have maximum flexibility in allocating funds among the various services."

The task force placed special emphasis upon strengthening state and local suppliers of manpower services, in order to give the potential client a "one-stop service center." The major objective was a planning and delivery system that was state and local in its basis, with federal monitoring to assure standards. Building on the CAMPS experience, states (and possibly large metropolitan areas) would be required to prepare and update plans for using their manpower dollars. Planning would be the responsibility of elected officials, though "all relevant interests, public and private, should have access to the planners." State and local planning

[2] National Manpower Policy Task Force, *The Nation's Manpower Programs* (Washington, D.C., January 7, 1969).

12

should be centralized and augmented, though delivery agencies themselves need not be centralized. A portion of the congressional appropriations, perhaps as much as 30 percent, would be left in the hands of federal administrators to serve populations that have been neglected by states or communities, and to engage in research and technical assistance.

The ultimate objective of the reorganizations would be a single agency or even individual to represent the client and his manpower needs. "Each community should have a single contact point within reach of each individual, to dispense all services, or refer the individual to places where needed employability services can be obtained." An individual's eligibility would be determined by demographic characteristics rather than whether he fit into some narrow program category.

These two pronouncements were not the first expressions of reformist sentiment, nor were their recommendations especially novel. They were important, however, because they summarized the conclusions of many of those who had observed the new manpower programs most carefully during their first decade. Moreover, the statements formed the starting point for legislative proposals and administrative experimentation during the next few years.

It should not be assumed, however, that this "consensus" view, as reflected in these two high level policy statements, was unanimously shared by federal bureaucrats down the line. The huge corps of workers who manage the federal establishment includes many who are steeped in the New Deal tradition and believe fervently in the wisdom and power of the national government. This is especially so in the Labor Department, a significant proportion of whose employees have been associated or at least identified with the labor movement. Many of these officials had devoted their efforts to involving the federal government in services at the local level, and thus were unwilling to see the authority which had been built up diminished in any way. Moreover, some program officials were (in the words of one of them) "discomforted" at the prospect that the current emphasis upon poor and disadvantaged workers might be abandoned at the hands of unresponsive governors or mayors.

Officials of the U.S. Training and Employment Service, in particular, were suspicious of any proposals which failed to acknowledge the state employment services as the prime planner and deliverer of manpower services. They viewed the emphasis upon elected officials as a challenge to the traditional preeminence of their agencies. Staff members in the Office of Education's Vocational Education Division held similar views about the treatment given their programs. As it turned out, however, neither of these groups played a large role in subsequent legislative reform efforts—either in drafting the administration's bill or in affecting subsequent outcomes on Capitol Hill.

The bulk of high level opinion in the Manpower Administration, not to mention its outside consultants, therefore favored consolidation and decentralization of manpower services. It was not lost upon these experts, moreover, that such an approach was likely to enjoy a favorable reception from the new Republican Administration.

A State-Oriented Solution

Credit for the first major legislative proposal to deal with these problems went to Representative William A. Steiger (R-Wis.), whose "Comprehensive Manpower Act" (H.R.10908) was introduced on May 5, 1969.[3] As a freshman congressman, Steiger and his legislative assistant, Peter Kobrak, had begun to delve into the topic during considerations of MDTA amendments the year before and had become convinced that drastic reorganization was needed. Working from the Mangum paper, the National Manpower Policy Task Force statement and numerous other sources, Steiger and Kobrak worked up a bill designed "to develop a systematic national manpower policy and to provide a comprehensive delivery

[3] Co-sponsors were Republican Representatives Albert Quie (Minn.), William Widnall (N. J.), John Erlenborn (Ill.), John Dellenback (Ore.), Edwin Eshleman (Penna.), and Orval Hansen (Idaho).

system for manpower services." It included several features which expert opinion favored for realigning manpower services: long-range manpower planning, program mixtures adapted to community circumstances, and packaging of services to fit individual needs—"one-stop shopping" for training, work experience, and placement services.

The Steiger bill envisioned essentially a federal-state relationship. The secretary of labor would enter into agreements with each governor to provide a full range of manpower services according to a state-developed plan. This state plan, developed only after public hearings, would then be approved by the governor and finally the secretary of labor. A major role would also be played, however, by a central state planning group established with the approval of the governor and the secretary of labor and including representatives from state education and employment agencies, not to mention labor, management, private manpower agencies, and the general public. The bill included numerous guidelines for the drafting of state manpower plans; and planning grants, and incentive grants to "resourceful and imaginative" states, were authorized to enhance state performance.

Several considerations lay behind this emphasis upon state governments. First, Steiger wanted manpower planning to be done on the basis of the largest possible geographic areas. The burgeoning literature on the administrative problems, moreover, tended to stress the states as promising but unused partners. Finally, Steiger intended to add a "pass-through" provision of some kind, a guarantee of manpower funds to certain types of localities under specified conditions. But few experts had ready ideas for the design of such a feature, and Steiger was in a hurry to put his bill into the hopper as soon as possible. So the proposal was drafted with the states as prime sponsors, the intention being that a provision pertaining to localities could be added later in the legislative process.

Though the plan awarded a preeminent role to the states, the federal government was empowered to regulate and monitor the system. Seventy percent of the authorized funds (which would range from $2 billion in fiscal 1971 to $3 billion in fiscal 1974) were to be allotted to the states according to formula; 30 percent would be reserved for the secretary's use. The department would be responsible for special programs for low-income and chronically unemployed workers—in addition to research, demonstration, and evaluation programs. The federal government would also help the states by providing training for personnel and other technical assistance. HEW was authorized to supervise and evaluate all instructional training.

The Steiger bill envisioned a streamlined system of the federal-state relationships. As it turned out, however, its extreme reliance upon the state governments was a serious political liability; and while the bill included some innovations carried into later debates, the federal-state structure was never really given serious consideration.

A NATIONAL SOLUTION

Three weeks later, on May 26, there appeared a second man-power reform measure: the "Manpower Act" (H.R.11620), introduced by six-term Representative James G. O'Hara (D-Mich.), who had long been regarded as the liberal Democrats' chief spokes-man on manpower legislation. Floor leader for every major man-power bill since the original MDTA in 1962, he was widely recognized as a master of legislative strategy and tactics. As spokesman for a blue-collar constituency, O'Hara advocated vigorous government job creation efforts in periods of economic decline. As a friend of urban and labor interests, O'Hara had little confidence in state prerogatives; rather, he believed that the federal government, as the funding source, should retain strong control over the goals and standards of manpower programs. In refining his views and drafting his bill, O'Hara was advised by Dr. Curt Aller, an economics professor who had previously served as staff director for the Select Labor Subcommittee.

The O'Hara bill reflected these political considerations remark-ably well. It envisioned decategorization but by no means decentralization. In fact, the O'Hara bill was the most national of all the proposals for manpower reform. According to the proposal, the secretary of labor would be responsible for providing training and other manpower services—directly or through contracts with any public or private agency. There was no requirement for concurrent approval by other federal agencies, or for utilizing any particular state or local agencies. Maximum flexibility was provided. The secretary was simply empowered to select the most economical, efficient mode of operation to provide services on a nondiscriminatory basis, tailored to individual needs, convenient for participants, and appropriate in standards. No dollar amounts were attached, and no proportions set up among the various types of manpower services. Although the secretary of labor was given full responsibility, the authorization was placed on a two-year basis to facilitate congressional review.

O'Hara's bill embraced the usual range of manpower services, with two important additions. A public-service employment program was authorized by Title III, whereby the secretary would contract with any governmental or private organization to provide jobs for unemployed workers. The workers were to be paid the prevailing wage along with various benefits. Title II placed emphasis on programs for upgrading the skills and pay of workers already in the labor force. Consistent with these programs, the measure stated its objectives in spacious terms: "to guarantee every American willing and able to work, an opportunity for a meaningful job and for training."

The Administration Drafts a Bill

Soon after the Nixon administration assumed office, the White House staff canvassed the departments for domestic program suggestions. Because of the time a comprehensive manpower bill would require to get through Congress, Shultz and Weber proposed to revamp the delivery of services within the existing legislative framework (a long-awaited internal reorganization plan was just being implemented). The White House responded, however, by asking for new legislation: both the president and his senior domestic counselor, economist Arthur F. Burns, were on record in favor of manpower reform, and at the time the president was being criticized in the press for tardiness in putting forward a legislative program. Thus the Labor Department was directed to draft an administration manpower bill. When the Manpower Training Act was finally sent to Congress on August 12, 1969, it stood with the Family Assistance Plan (FAP) and revenue-sharing as symbolic pillars of the president's "new federalism." Although touted by the White House and the press as part of the president's program, the manpower bill contained essentially the consensus views about manpower organization that had been developing for several years. Thus MTA was a happy marriage of traditional Republican philosophy and expert opinion within the manpower policy community.

MTA would have consolidated the remedial manpower programs of MDTA, EOA (except for the Job Corps), and the employment service. Three-quarters of the funds were to be apportioned among the states, with the remainder used by the department for national activities and incentive payments to states demonstrating "exemplary performance." On the state level, governors would designate a "prime sponsor"—to plan and administer the programs—and approve an annual state plan for utilizing manpower funds. At the local level, prime sponsors would be designated by the governors from units of local general governments. But if the head of a unit (or units) of local government representing at least 75 percent of the area's population concurred in nominating another agency (public or private) as prime sponsor, the governor was required to designate this nominee. In either case, the prime sponsor would be subject to approval by the secretary of labor. The prime sponsor provision (Title I) was designed by Labor Department drafters to deal with the problem of multiple local governmental jurisdictions, and at the same time to encourage prime sponsors to represent the largest possible labor-market area. To allay urban officials' fears that they would be treated unfairly by the states, the bill included a pass-through provision guaranteeing each metropolitan area its minimum share of the state's apportionment—based on its share of the state's labor force and disadvantaged individuals.

For those who were squeamish about abandoning manpower programs to state or local units of government, the bill set up a three-step process whereby prime sponsors could gain full funding for their proposed programs. Moreover, if a local prime sponsor's plan of service was vetoed at the state level, it could be appealed to the secretary, who would then determine who was correct. The secretary also retained extensive powers to approve or disapprove state or local plans. Thus MTA was designed as a streamlined federal grant program, emphasizing decentralization to state and local governments but providing safeguards for those interests which thought they would fare better with the federal establishment.

In sending MTA to Congress, President Nixon declared that it "would pull together much of the array of federal training services and make it possible for state and local government to respond to the needs of the individual trainee." As a part of the administration's new federalism package, MTA initially drew wide support among leading Republicans in both houses.[4]

SUMMARY

These three manpower reorganization proposals served as points of departure for an investigation of the manpower "delivery system" during the 91st Congress. The proposals stemmed from the growing sense of uneasiness over the effectiveness of federal aid programs, and reflected a growing feeling within a manpower community that "something must be done" to consolidate and streamline programs. But the bills differed radically in their approach to the institutions and process of federalism. If these issues were not enough to cloud the future of the manpower subgovernment, the O'Hara bill posed still another and potentially even more

[4] The bill (S.2838, H.R.13472) was introduced by Senator Jacob K. Javits (N.Y.) and Representative William Ayres (Ohio), ranking members of the relevant congressional committees.

explosive issue: the government's role in actually creating jobs for those unable to compete in the private sector labor market. Here was an issue which had divided liberals and conservatives historically since the New Deal, and which could be counted upon to produce fierce debate in times of high unemployment.

As significant as what was said about decategorization, however, was the parade of witnesses who came before the subcommittee to extol categorical programs in which they were involved. Categorical interests were most visible during the day of hearings devoted to the Opportunities Industrialization Centers (OIC), a movement which began in an abandoned Philadelphia jailhouse in 1964 and had since grown into a comprehensive manpower program providing skill training, remedial education, job placement, and supportive services to its recruits. Under the charismatic direction of the Reverend Leon H. Sullivan, the Philadelphia OIC prototype had spread to 90 communities throughout the nation. By 1970 the OIC's received about $50 million annually from the federal government (from Labor, HEW, and OEO) but had no specific statutory recognition. A bipartisan group of senators introduced a proposal (Amendment 440) to assure that OIC's would be eligible for federal funds under MTA, both on a local and a national basis. After Reverend Sullivan spoke to the subcommittee and showed an inspirational film on OIC's work, Javits promised that "as the principal sponsor of the administration's manpower bill . . . I want to say that Amendment 440 will, of course, be a part of our bill." No less than nine senators and an equal number of representatives were on hand to record their praise for OIC's. Minority leader Hugh Scott (R-Penna.), took time off from Senate floor debate to appear and urge a single funding source for OIC under the manpower bill. "I want you to know I am one of your missionaries," he told Sullivan.[9] All in all, it was a bad day for the concept of decategorization.

DECENTRALIZE TO WHOM?

The related notion of decentralizing planning and decisionmaking to the states received an even cooler reception from witnesses. The senators doubted that conflicts could be avoided in designating prime sponsors, and felt that cities would be discriminated against.

[9] *Senate Hearings*, 3; 1173.

"Our intent," Shultz explained in an appearance before the sub-committee, "is that the mayor of the metropolitan area's dominant city should be the presumptive choice for the prime sponsor."[10] Again, verbal assurance from the secretary did not satisfy the legislators.

After generations of neglect of urban problems, the state governments were simply not trusted to play such a pivotal role in manpower programs. Poor people, community action workers, program officials, mayors, and labor spokesmen told the subcommittee of the shoddy treatment which needy clients had received at the hands of state agencies. "The state houses," Mayor Joseph Alioto of San Francisco declared, ". . . don't have that sensitivity with the problems of the big cities."[11]

Specifically, many people feared that the states would delegate their responsibilities to the employment services, which they castigated as unresponsive, bureaucratic, and slow. A Chicano leader from Los Angeles explained that "dealing with the state employment service has been a horrendous experience . . . especially for the client who is subjected to the most exasperating and demeaning process that completely strips a person of his dignity."[12] Representative Shirley Chisholm (D-N.Y.) received a standing ovation after she tore into the record of the employment service. "The whole reason manpower programs came into existence in the first place," she declared, "is that the state employment services were not doing their jobs. It seems ludicrous to me to reward them for their failure just because it fits someone's philosophical scheme of decentralization."[13] Criticism was so persistent that the subcommittee scheduled a day of hearings to allow employment service officials to defend themselves. The session ended in a virtual rout for the state officials as Chairman Nelson, himself a former governor, worked them over with a barrage of questions. "I don't understand, quite frankly," he declared, "how you can give signifi-

---

[10] *Senate Hearings*, 4; 2825.
[11] *Senate Hearings*, 3; 1623.
[12] *Senate Hearings*, 1; 421.
[13] *Senate Hearings*, 3; 1108.

cant authority to an agency which is rejected totally by all of the groups to be served." The witnesses protested that their own agencies were innocent of the charges but, as one of them conceded, "the testimony that you might have received is certainly understandable."[14]

Urban interests were united in opposing the state role envisioned in the administration's bill. The U.S. Conference of Mayors–League of Cities, a large and effective Washington lobby, organized effective pressures and recruited a number of mayors and other urban officials to testify on manpower problems in their communities. This proved an easy task, for considerable groundwork had already been laid. In 1969 the Labor Department had launched a quiet program to involve the mayors through a series of grants, first to the Conference of Mayors for a series of conferences and studies, and then under CAMPS planning funds to mayors themselves for manpower coordinating staffs in the local communities. As a result, mayors and their staffs were gaining new interest and expertise in local manpower programs, and they saw manpower reorganization as a means of capturing new funds and garnering potential political credit.

The mayors' spokesmen were joined by community action officials. It appeared, in fact, that relations between city halls and antipoverty agencies had grown more cordial than the poverty program's critics had realized. No doubt the shared distrust of state agencies had helped to foster the détente.[15] Whatever the

[14] Ibid., pp. 1271–72.

[15] The distrust was fueled by a long-standing dispute between the Department of Labor and OEO concerning the respective roles of employment services and CAA's in the manpower field. According to a 1968 memorandum of agreement between the two agencies, CAA's were to be "presumptive prime sponsors" and the employment services "presumptive providers of services." OEO and its supporters believed that the Department of Labor was construing these powers unfairly in a series of guidelines for the Concentrated Employment Program (CEP). Disagreement between the Labor Department and OEO also produced a stalemate over how to implement Title I-B of the Economic Opportunity Act, which contemplated manpower coordination. Nelson and other pro-OEO legislators made certain that the Labor Department's role was fully criticized during the hearings.

reasons, scores of antipoverty workers came forward to argue for local representation in programming planning and implementation; their arguments were backed by lengthy briefs prepared by the National Association for Community Development, a group begun in 1965 as a kind of "clientele group" for community action agencies.

Meanwhile, spokesmen for the states hardly put in an appearance. By all logic the governors should have played a vigorous lobbying role, since the proposed legislation could have benefited them greatly. Staff members at the National Governors' Conference tried vainly to mobilize the governors on this issue, preferably in support of some version of the Steiger bill. Labor Department officials, whose bill hinged upon statewide coordination, tried also to involve the governors. All these efforts were fruitless. The governors made no efforts to influence the drafting of the legislation; and while the employment security directors were on the firing line, only one governor made it to Capitol Hill to discuss the manpower bill.[16] Lacking support from the governors, the Interstate Conference of Employment Security Agencies (ICESA) remained relatively quiet until very late in the game.

Why were the governors so ineffective when they had so much at stake? A combination of factors was involved. Despite the long-standing involvement of state agencies in manpower services, very few of the governors had intimate knowledge of manpower problems. Most state employment security agencies operate with considerable independence from control by elected state officials, executive or legislative. When CAMPS planning grants were awarded the states to foster centralized coordination under the governors' aegis, more often than not the governors simply turned the responsibilities over to the employment services. Thus, with a few exceptions, the governors proved less knowledgeable and interested than their local rivals—the mayors, community action officials, and representatives of the disadvantaged.

[16] This was Calvin Rampton of Utah. See U.S. House of Representatives, Select Subcommittee on Labor, *Manpower Act of 1969*, 91st Cong., 2nd sess., 1970, 2; 1313–26.

Within the Governors' Conference, the Human Resources Committee (one of six policymaking committees) discusses manpower issues but does not consider them its primary concern. To the extent the governors considered the issue at all, they tended to assume that the states should have total responsibility for all manpower services. As one high administration official put it, "the governors got greedy, and because of that they got nothing." At heart, the governors seemed unwilling to permit large-city mayors, as potential political rivals, to exercise such control over manpower programs. This reasoning seemed particularly influential with Governor Nelson Rockefeller, a political rival of Mayor John Lindsay of New York City. As chairman of the Human Resources Committee, Rockefeller's lack of enthusiasm for the bill was a key factor in the inaction of the Governors' Conference.

The combination of urban strength and state weakness placed the administration in a difficult position. The authors of MTA believed they had devised a judicious balance between the prerogatives of the states and localities. One of them described MTA as "a city bill in state clothing." This view is open to debate: on the one hand, we have seen that the administration's bill was not intended as a vehicle for aggrandizement by the employment services; yet it is hard to see why it would not have turned out that way in a number of states. The governors, as potential allies of MTA, had badly misread the situation; and their Washington lobbyists, who knew the score, were frustrated at not being able to mobilize their clients. Politically, the question was not whether the governors could be given more power than the administration had offered them, but whether the states could possibly obtain that much power. The activist urban lobbies set about making certain that Congress would write language to guarantee urban control over manpower money distributed in their areas. Having failed in two high-level meetings to persuade the governors to take action, Labor Department strategists were ultimately forced to abandon the governors and accept the political solution drafted on Capitol Hill.

Concern over representation of local groups resulted in one

solid innovation gleaned from the hearings. This came from Hugh Calkins, chairman of the National Advisory Council on Vocational Education, in the form of a suggestion for a local level manpower commission to be chaired by the mayor with participants from schools, community colleges, and other government agencies with a role in manpower. Such an agency would formulate its plans with the advice of broader advisory committees, including representatives of the poor, the business community, and labor unions. Presumably the pattern could be used on the state level as well. The idea found its way into the eventual Senate bill.[17]

PUBLIC SERVICE JOBS

Not since the 1930s had the federal government sponsored any large scale activities designed explicitly to create jobs and put vast numbers of unemployed workers to work. As the bleak memories of the Depression faded from view, New Deal job efforts began to be remembered disparagingly as "leaf-raking" or "make-work" programs. But two developments refocused attention upon the government's potential role in job creation. Unemployment and underemployment were becoming an acute problem among ghetto area residents—even during the generalized prosperity of the 1960s. A second development was the mounting feeling that services, especially those in urban and rural poverty communities, were falling increasingly behind the needs.[18] In 1966 the Commission on Technology, Automation, and Economic Progress urged that the government be considered the "employer of last resort," and estimated that 5.3 million jobs could be filled in the public sector. Two years later an Urban Coalition report estimated that about 280,000 jobs could be created in the 50 cities having

[17] *Senate Hearings*, 1; 715–17.
[18] See *Technology and the American Economy*, Report of the National Commission on Technology, Automation and Economic Progress (Washington, D.C.: Government Printing Office, 1966), esp. pp. 35–37, 110; Harold L. Sheppard, *The Nature of the Job Problem and the Role of New Public Service Employment* (Kalamazoo, Mich.: W. E. Upjohn Institute for Employment Research, January 1969), esp. pp. 24–25.

populations of 100,000 or more, and the Kerner Commission recommended a three-year program for creating one million public-sector jobs. Other task forces and commissions became interested in public-sector job creation, and by 1969 it was a major concern of such groups as the Urban Coalition, AFL-CIO, and the League of Cities–U.S. Conference of Mayors.

The public jobs issue was not a new one for Nelson. As author in 1965 of the so-called Nelson Amendment to the Economic Opportunity Act—the Operation Mainstream program to provide jobs on conservation projects for unemployed or underemployed workers—he said of the Administration's MTA proposals that they were "progressive . . . in some areas" but "fall awfully short." He charged that they "continue to emphasize training when enough jobs simply are not there." He announced his subcommittee's hearings as a means of seeking support for "a major program to create hundreds of thousands of public service employment jobs."[19]

Nelson found ample support for the public jobs concept, especially as unemployment rose.

Urban spokesmen had long been interested in getting federal assistance for public-service programs in urban areas, and they came through strongly for the idea during congressional hearings. The prepared statement of the National League of Cities–U.S. Conference of Mayors stated:

In most central cities, the unmet need of local government to provide greatly increased services and the continuing dangerously high level of unemployment (even during periods of prosperity) constitutes persuasive evidence for federal support of a public service employment program.[20]

Similarly, the President of the National Civil Service League stated:

We believe government as "employer of the first resort" can provide meaningful career opportunities for many who are unemployed and underemployed and at the same time, help meet severe staff shortages.[21]

[19] Press Release, September 1, 1969.
[20] *Senate Hearings*, 4; 3027.
[21] *Senate Hearings*, 3; 1413.

Support for public-service jobs was also heard from representatives of the AFL-CIO; the American Federation of State, County, and Municipal Employees; the Urban Coalition Action Council; and other groups. Mayors and other local officials documented the thousands of unfilled public-sector jobs in their communities. Meanwhile (and hardly by accident), the senators received glowing reports of such job creation programs as Nelson's Operation Mainstream and its Green Thumb component.[22]

Even Secretary Shultz acknowledged that "the broad support for some form of public service employment program has been an impressive result in these hearings."[23] But Shultz remained implacably opposed, taking the stance that broad monetary and fiscal measures, coupled with the limited job creation efforts linked to training, would be sufficient to curb cyclical unemployment. Curiously, however, he did not make clear the depth of his opposition to the notion, instead remarking to Senator Javits—who brought up the subject—that "I think we are all perhaps on the same track here."[24] Shultz's views on the issue were not explored in depth, a fact which was to assume decisive significance later on.

Two Senators, Ten Proxies

Using the hearings to corroborate their general ideas, Nelson's three-man subcommittee staff put together an "Employment and Training Opportunities Act" (S.3867), which Nelson and seven Democratic colleagues introduced just before the hearings ended. In authorizing virtually *any* manpower service, the proposal met the test of a comprehensive manpower bill. In other respects, however, it bore little resemblance to MTA. Any unit of local general government was eligible to become a prime sponsor, and community action agencies were guaranteed a role. A multibillion

[22] *Senate Hearings*, 4; 25–27.
[23] Ibid., p. 2830.
[24] Ibid., p. 2831.

dollar public-service program was included as Title I. There were separate titles for other specific programs such as Nelson's own environmental projects, OIC's and youth programs. In writing the bill, Nelson's staff had worked to incorporate the interests of other committee Democrats.

Once the hearings were ended, Nelson's bill became the basis for negotiations within the subcommittee—both informally and in the mark-up sessions, where the bill is formally worked on. Actually, Nelson and his staff were embroiled in two sets of negotiations. On the one hand, other Democrats on the subcommittee insisted that the bill assure a role for categorical interests. At the insistence of Alan Cranston (D-Calif.), community action agencies were given stronger guarantees of a voice in planning and implementing local manpower programs. To "guarantee that a number of relatively unique and vital programs are maintained," special provisions were added for mid-career and elderly people (Jennings Randolph of West Virginia and Harrison Williams of New Jersey); for Indians (Edward Kennedy of Massachusetts); and for Spanish-speaking people (Ralph Yarborough of Texas). A community environment service was included at the suggestion of Nelson's office staff. Needless to mention, the OIC's were given special recognition in the bill.

By engaging in the time-honored tactic of logrolling, Nelson and his staff (in truth, most negotiations in the Senate take place at the staff level) managed to build an unshakable coalition of the subcommittee's majority party members. Some of the provisions represented clear constituency concerns of the senators—for example, mid-career development for the depressed regions of West Virginia or Spanish-language programs for the Texas border country. Other concerns, however, were manifestations of broader, nongeographic roles cultivated by the senators. There are few Indians in Massachusetts, but no doubt it was to enhance Kennedy's reputation as a champion of minority groups that his staff became a conduit for the view of the Indian lobby. Likewise, Nelson's reputation as an environmentalist was in the minds of his staff. This type of policy entrepreneurship is widespread in the Senate, as opposed to the committee specialization so familiar in the House. As we will see the result was to make the Senate the voice of demographic clienteles while House committee members were more responsive to the technical constituency within the manpower community and hence more apt to reflect the thinking of professionals and experts in the field.

On a second front, Nelson was negotiating with Javits, who was more or less representing the administration's position. As one of the most liberal Senate Republicans and a previous sponsor of public-service jobs plans, Javits found himself closer to Nelson than to the administration and presented most of the latter's suggested amendments with less than full enthusiasm. Javits was able to win some concessions on the public-service employment program, in the form of amendments linking the programs with on-the-job training and assuring that workers would not be allowed to remain permanently in subsidized jobs. But on most of the major issues—the general contours of public-service jobs, the role of the states and localities, and the continuation of categorical programs—Javits could not or would not, budge the majority Nelson had put together. Most of the mark-up sessions were attended only by Nelson and Javits, with issues being resolved when Javits' four proxy votes were overcome by Nelson's six proxies. In the end, Javits felt he had obtained the best compromise he could, and thus he supported the revised S.3867. On August 20, the full Labor and Public Welfare Committee voted to report the bill. The only dissenting votes were cast by the three conservative Republicans. Javits and two GOP colleagues, Winston Prouty (Vt.) and Richard Schweiker (Penna.), accepted the bill with reservations.[25] Soon afterwards, the full Labor and Public Welfare Committee met and, with very little debate, voted to report S.3867. The three GOP senators who had filed supplemental views to the subcommittee's report were the only dissenters.

[25] U.S. Senate, Committee on Labor and Public Welfare, *Employment and Training Opportunities Act of 1970*, S. Rept. 91–1136, 91st Cong., 2nd sess., 1970.

Senate Floor Passage

When Nelson's S.3867 went to the Senate floor in mid-September, the administration found itself in a quandary. The measure was not at all what they wanted; the initial feeling was that "the bill was so bad that nothing could be done to it or for it." Yet administration officials had kept hands off the negotiations—partly out of deference to Javits, partly because of a hiatus caused by personnel changes in the Labor Department. Meanwhile Javits had lost whatever enthusiasm he might have held for MTA, and after the negotiations became a strong supporter of the revised Nelson bill. But even had Javits been a more forceful advocate of the administration's position, he would have lost all the major battles. Finally, on the eve of the Senate floor debate, Malcolm Lovell, the new assistant secretary for manpower, decided to commit himself to obtaining an acceptable manpower bill, and he obtained White House clearance for a series of amendments to be offered on the floor. Since Javits was now supporting the Nelson bill, Lovell called upon Peter Dominick (R-Colo.) to present the administration's case on the floor.

Lovell's decision had the effect of committing the administration at long last to public-service employment—since the department's series of amendments was designed to tighten but not eliminate this portion of the Nelson bill. The Nixon administration's gradual acceptance of this position was aided by both personal and political forces. Shultz and his assistant secretary, Arnold Weber, had always been opposed to the concept on principle; but their successors, Secretary James Hodgson and Lovell, viewed the matter more pragmatically. Thus they asked for, and received, the tacit assent of the White House to accept public-service jobs in the form of the Dominick amendments. No doubt the overpowering consideration at the White House was the fact that national unemployment was above five percent with the congressional elections looming ahead. But the image of "make-work" jobs still haunted many GOP leaders, and clearly Lovell's room for bargaining was severely limited.

Nelson described S.3867 on the Senate floor as a measure which achieved the Nixon administration's objectives of streamlining and decentralizing manpower services.[26] Special programs—the "something for everybody" which had initially shocked administration officials—were characterized as "badly needed special programs for persons not ordinarily served by conventional manpower programs." Nelson was able to characterize the bill as a bipartisan measure which had "won the support of a major coalition of interested and well-informed citizens, concerned about joblessness and idleness on the one hand, and the steady deterioration and decay of our communities on the other hand."

The administration's series of six amendments was presented on the floor by Senator Dominick, who had the benefit of only a few hours' preparation. Three of the amendments were debated in some detail: one would have eliminated the categorization of funds by eliminating the one-third distribution of funds among manpower services, public-service jobs, and special programs; another would have strengthened the governors' role by giving them something very close to a veto power over manpower plans emanating from metropolitan areas; the third would have assured that public-service jobs were temporary, by imposing a two-year limit and restricting trainees' salaries to 80 percent of the prevailing weekly wage (or, if higher, the prevailing minimum wage). All three amendments were beaten badly by a coalition of Democrats and liberal Republicans.[27]

Significantly, however, Dominick won Nelson's agreement to accept one amendment—which provided explicit authority for the secretary to use his own funds to effectuate any title in the bill. Although seemingly innocuous, this amendment would have given the Labor Department much of the flexibility its strategists wanted to break out of categorical funding. After that concession, Dominick, knowing that the battle was lost, informed the Senate that he

[26] Senate debate on S.3827 appears in *Congressional Record*, daily ed., September 16–17, 1970, pp. S15720–70, S15856–912.

[27] Votes on the amendments were 19–55, 28–46, and 29–43, respectively.

would not call up the remaining two administration amendments and stated, "I am through for the day."

At the conclusion of the floor debate, S.3867 was passed by an overwhelming 68–6 vote, with only a handful of conservative Republicans voting nay. Javits told the Senate that "notwithstanding our differences" over public-service employment, S.3867 was "a monumental measure in the manpower training field."

Nelson's measure was a broad-ranging though somewhat confusing document. It authorized extensive reorganization and clearly committed the government to the controversial role of "employer of last resort." But the complex funding requirements for categories of clients would have made the measure difficult to implement. Nelson was able to sell S.3867 as a bipartisan measure supported by nearly everyone, perhaps even by the administration. One inexperienced Nixon appointee had warned Nelson's subcommittee staff director not to report out a bill with so many categorical programs. "You'll be the laughing stock of everyone," the administration aide protested. "Why, there is something for everybody in that bill!" The remark occasioned much laughter around Nelson's office, for of course that was the very reason for the bill's attractiveness.

4

Compromise in the House

By anyone's standard, the House of Representatives with its 435 members is a sizable legislative body. From this simple fact stem most of the differences between the House and Senate. Rather than representing a large and heterogeneous statewide constituency, the representative speaks for a district which is likely to be more homogeneous in its legislative demands. Individual legislators in the House can afford to concentrate their efforts on one or two issue areas. The two principal manpower negotiators in the Senate, Nelson and Javits, had no less than nine committee assignments between them; in addition, Nelson chaired two subcommittees while Javits was nominally ranking minority member of nine. In the House, in contrast, two of the three primary negotiators had only one committee assignment; the third was member of another committee in which he had secondary interest. Thus individual representatives, while commanding fewer staff resources than their Senate counterparts, can often find time to become acknowledged experts on public policy questions.

Another difference in the two houses, at least in recent years, has been their differing positions on general public policy matters. In a word, the Senate as an institution has become more liberal than the House. The reasons for this fact arise mainly from the fact that a senator's constituency—an entire state—is more varied, and thus more likely to have large numbers of urban voters, than the smaller constituency of the congressman.[1] Congressional Democrats had agreed tacitly to allow the more liberal Senate to take the lead on manpower legislation; now, however, the powerful "conservative coalition" of partisan Republicans and conservative Democrats on the House floor would have to be faced.

Set against this background, the House Education and Labor Committee is an especially controversial arena for decisionmaking. Its jurisdiction embraces many of the ideological issues which have divided liberals and conservatives since the New Deal era. The committee thus attracts Democratic liberals, who want to have a hand in framing strong legislation in these fields; conservatives, in contrast, tend to find their way to other committees, including those dealing with taxing and budgeting. This leaves the committee's majority significantly more liberal in outlook than the House as a whole. This phenomenon is demonstrated by extracting liberalism scores from the voting studies prepared by *Congressional Quarterly*.[2] In 1970, for example, members of the Education and Labor Committee scored an average of 50 percent on the index, compared to 33 percent for the House as a whole; Democrats on the committee scored 71 percent, compared to only 45 percent for all House Democrats. Committee Republicans, on the other hand, were only slightly more conservative than the House Republicans as a whole. Divisiveness within the committee, and between the committee and the parent house, was an important underlying factor in the subsequent course of manpower reform legislation.

[1] See Lewis A. Froman, *Congressmen and their Constituencies* (Chicago: Rand McNally, 1963), chap. 6.

[2] Our liberalism index is derived from "conservative coalition" votes on the House floor. The coalition is an alliance of Republicans and southern Democrats—that is, when a majority of voting Republicans and southern Democrats oppose a stand taken by a majority of voting northern Democrats. For the present purpose, we have compiled the percentage of conservative coalition roll calls on which the Member voted *in disagreement* with the coalition. Hence, we use the index as a rough indicator of liberalism. The index is recorded in *Congressional Quarterly Weekly Report*, January 29, 1971, pp. 242–47.

As the Nelson bill was approved by the Senate, manpower legislation was still pending in the House Education and Labor Committee. Between December 1969 and May 1970, Dominick V. Daniels' (D-N.J.) Select Labor Subcommittee had conducted 27 days of hearings in Washington and elsewhere. These inquiries covered much the same ground as the Senate hearings, and uncovered many of the same findings—support for public-service employment, acceptance in principle of reorganization of manpower services, and solicitude over traditional manpower programs. The tone of the hearings, however, was somewhat more favorable to the administration's proposals and their concepts of decategorization and decentralization.[3]

When the Nelson bill was passed, Democratic members of Daniels' subcommittee were holding a series of secret caucuses, from which Republicans were excluded.[4] The Democrats were in the process of deciding to support a pure public-service employment bill (H.R.19377) introduced by O'Hara—who had by this time abandoned manpower reorganization. Under the circumstances, the Democrats' move could only be reckoned a gamble. Given the conservatism of the House and its leadership, it was quite uncertain whether the House would pass a public-service employment bill, or even whether the Rules Committee would allow such a bill onto the floor. Moreover, time was running out on the 91st Congress; and in an election year members, impatient to return to the hustings, spend less and less time in Washington. The pressure of time and the difficulty of obtaining quorums work to the advantage of those who oppose a piece of legislation; and with the controversy which would undoubtedly be stirred by a public-service bill, these liabilities could ill be afforded. Such a

---

[3] U.S. House of Representatives, Committee on Education and Labor, Select Subcommittee on Labor, *Manpower Act of 1969*, 91st Cong., 2nd sess., 1970, in two parts. In addition to the Washington hearings, the Subcommittee—like its Senate counterpart—traveled to several cities to hear testimony.

[4] Since early in the 91st Congress, committee sessions were open to the press and the public. This practice was accompanied, however, by closed partisan caucuses prior to committee sessions.

bill might obtain committee approval, but it would need broader support to have any real chance of passage.

THE "PUMPKIN PAPERS"

The lines were drawn, and compromise seemed out of the question within the limited time remaining. But the two sides were closer than it appeared at first glance. At a manpower researchers' conference late in September, Representative Steiger indicated that he favored working with the Nelson bill to remedy its defects. He warned that a straight public-service jobs bill had little chance of passage, and S.3867, as passed by the Senate, was unacceptable. Yet he indicated he was prepared to accept some type of public-service employment—though in neither the form nor the funding level provided in the Senate bill. Emphasizing that the issues of public jobs and manpower reorganization were inextricably interlocked, he invited the Democrats to start negotiating with "mutuality of interests." "Do we want a good bill," he asked, "or do we simply want a political issue?"

Speaking at the same session, Representative O'Hara delivered a rousing stump speech in favor of public-service jobs, indicating he was unwilling to stall the subcommittee with manpower reorganization at such a late date in the session. "Reorganization is fine, and I have been for this from the very beginning," he noted. "But we have already acted, and nothing happens," referring to Title I-B of the 1967 Economic Opportunity Act amendments. Choosing his words with care, O'Hara conceded that the subcommittee Democrats were "considering" reporting a pure public-sector employment bill—a tip-off that the barn door had not entirely been blocked. He promised that public jobs would be integrated into the totality of manpower programs and that they would be real, regular jobs. As for the administration's amendments which would have limited such jobs to two years and 80 percent of the prevailing wage, he replied: "I can't accept that, any more than I would accept making the enrollees wear some sort of a badge on the job."

Downtown at the Labor Department, the new assistant secretary, Malcolm Lovell, and his aides were confronted with another difficult choice. If the O'Hara public jobs bill passed the House, it would go to conference with the Nelson bill, thus yielding some combination of the two unacceptable measures. If the O'Hara bill failed, the lateness of the congressional session made it virtually impossible for any manpower bill at all to be enacted. As he reviewed the situation, Lovell became more and more convinced that a manpower bill from the 91st Congress would be desirable. The Economic Opportunity Act would probably face a bitter fight for renewal the following year; from the department's standpoint, it would be useful to have already shifted the manpower titles from EOA to a comprehensive manpower act. Moreover, it was not lost on Lovell and his staff that a bargain was possible: O'Hara needed bipartisan support in the House for his legislation, and only the administration could provide it. The administration, for its part, needed a vehicle for manpower reorganization. The bargain would hinge upon finding acceptable language for a public-service employment provision—language that would fuse O'Hara's insistence on "real, regular jobs" with the conservatives' desire to avoid "make-work" jobs.

For once, the administration acted swiftly and decisively. Because the House members were unlikely to give detailed examination to the 166-page Nelson bill, it was reasoned that a new proposal—one that did not have the imprint of various senators—would be more attractive. Within a few hours of the O'Hara-Steiger speeches, one of Lovell's aides, David Rusk, was hard at work putting together a "clean bill" which embodied and consolidated several existing legislative proposals, primarily the original O'Hara bill (H.R.11620), the Nelson bill (S.3867), the administration's proposed amendments, and the Steiger bill (H.R.10908). A day later, the document was in the hands of Steiger and Jim Harrison, O'Hara's manpower aide. "In my judgment," Rusk told Harrison, "if it is acceptable to you, it will be acceptable to the Labor Department." Because the draft had no official standing as an administration position, and at first had not been reviewed by policymakers with the authority to make such decisions, the document was referred to as "the pumpkin papers," reminiscent of the clandestine documents from the Alger Hiss-Whittaker Chambers era.

A few days later, Lovell was able to use a private meeting with labor and urban lobbyists to get across the message that (a) department policymakers really wanted a manpower bill; (b) if they could obtain manpower reorganization, they would accept public-service employment; and (c) although the proposed amendments to the Nelson bill were still considered the basis for discussion, the underlying principles were more important than the specific provisions. The urban spokesmen were urged to talk with O'Hara and persuade him to negotiate with the administration. The lobbyists immediately complied with the request, and O'Hara agreed to sit down with administration representatives the next day.

The matter of timing was crucial: the morning of the day scheduled for the meeting, the Daniels subcommittee met to approve H.R.19377, O'Hara's revised public-service jobs bill. The vote was unanimous, with Republican members boycotting the session. During the vote on H.R.19377, however, O'Hara informed his Democratic colleagues that he was going to talk that afternoon with the Republicans to see if a compromise manpower bill could be devised. The whole venture was quite speculative, however, since the full Education and Labor Committee was scheduled to meet the very next morning to report out the O'Hara bill.

When the meeting began, the principal participants were Lovell, Steiger, O'Hara, and a more senior Republican representative, Albert Quie (Minn.).[5] After what one participant called "a half hour of painful groping," the negotiators turned to the issue of public-sector employment, and it was discovered that everyone agreed on general principles. The ice was broken, and the group began in earnest to mark up H.R.19377, O'Hara's just-introduced

---

[5] The meeting, which took place on September 29, was attended by about a dozen people. In addition to the principals—Lovell, O'Hara, Steiger, and Quie—there were staff representatives from labor, OMB, the Education and Labor Committee, and the offices of Steiger and O'Hara.

public-employment bill. O'Hara's insistence upon "real, regular jobs" was accepted, while the Labor Department negotiators had little difficulty gaining their objectives—a linkage between the subsidized jobs and other manpower programs, the establishment of objectives required of prime sponsors, and a stipulation that the secretary would reduce the federal contribution if the sponsor demonstrated that he could not move enrollees into unsubsidized jobs. Staff members left the room to "draft some language," which was then accepted by the principal bargainers. An administration representative phoned downtown to obtain a green light on the outlines of the emerging provision, and the log jam had been broken.

What had begun as a tentative exploration of views quickly turned into a no-nonsense bargaining session that lasted throughout the afternoon and late into the night. Later, when the discussion turned to manpower organization, the basic outlines of the Nelson bill could not be avoided. However, Steiger and the administration representatives succeeded in raising to 100,000 the minimum population figure for local prime sponsors. A residual category then had to be designed for Education and Labor Committee Chairman Carl Perkins (D-Ky.), who would be certain to insist that counties in his depressed eastern Kentucky constituency be able to run their own manpower programs without interference from the current governor. His staff aide presented language which would allow nonmetropolitan areas to band together and become prime sponsors for local delivery systems. For the administration's benefit, the concept of the state plan of services was beefed up by such devices as requiring integrated manpower services and expanding the governor's right to comment on locally designed plans. Moreover, various pieces of language in the bill would have given the secretary of labor latitude in fashioning a comprehensive planning mechanism.

When the categorical programs of S.3867 were discussed, the bargainers unanimously agreed that these should be eliminated as separate authorizations. On the other hand, the definition of manpower services was broadened to include language which obviously embraced the various categorical programs. An entire title (Title II) was devoted to occupational upgrading because O'Hara wanted it and the department had no objections. The program was intended to "assist private or public employers in meeting the costs of providing their employees with the education and skills training needed to qualify themselves for . . . better jobs."[6] This notion had a great deal of potential appeal, but few people had a clear idea of how it might be achieved.

The final major question, how to allocate funds among the various segments of the bill, again occasioned surprisingly few problems. Administration spokesmen agreed to guarantee 18.75 percent of the total authorization as a national floor for public-service employment. But they resisted tying every local prime sponsor to this formula, and O'Hara agreed.

The resulting bill, H.R.19519, was called the Comprehensive Manpower Act. It was compact, containing only 72 pages in contrast with the Senate bill's 166. Title I described a comprehensive list of manpower services which could be funded by the federal government. Each state and each city of 100,000 people or more would be eligible to apply for prime sponsorship of manpower programs. In addition, certain units of local general governments could qualify by joining together to acquire the population base of 100,000. The Perkins provision specified that a unit or units of local general governments in rural areas could be prime sponsors if the secretary determined that they were suffering from substantial out-migration and high unemployment. In short, "any unit of government which meets the basic qualifications is entitled to operate its own manpower programs."[7]

The public-service employment section (Title III) specified that subsidized jobs must be "justifiable," "not . . . 'second-rate,' " and "the same kind of jobs that other employees have." Incentives were provided to ensure that employers were upgrading the trainees into regular unsubsidized jobs. These incentives involved

[6] House Rept. 91–1557, 91st Cong., 2nd sess., October 5, 1970, p. 10.
[7] Ibid., p. 9.

... setting objectives, at a time a public service agreement is negotiated, for the movement of persons employed thereunder into public or private employment not supported by this Act. If the employer has not achieved the objectives of this agreement, the Secretary is directed to reduce the federal share in any continuation or extension of the agreement, unless he ascertains that the employer was without fault, or that economic conditions prevented him from achieving this objective.[8]

This feature later became a bone of contention in the House-Senate negotiations.

The remainder of the bill—Titles IV and V—provided for research and demonstration projects, a national computerized job bank, and cultivation of employment in federal grant-in-aid programs. Various apportionments of the funds were also made. Federal money would be apportioned "on a non-earmarked basis, in equitable fashion, to states and, within states, to local areas served by local prime sponsors."[9] Maximum flexibility was given to the secretary to adjust funding to changing economic conditions, with the one exception of the 18.75 percent minimum to be expended on public service employment. At least 70 percent of the funds used for the first three titles would be apportioned among the states and local areas; other funds would be distributed at the discretion of the secretary of labor.

Despite numerous minor flaws attributable to haste, H.R.19519 was a source of pride for virtually everyone involved in the negotiations. Hours after the meeting broke up, Labor Secretary James Hodgson hailed the bill "a responsible response to President Nixon's request for comprehensive manpower legislation and . . . consonant with the basic principles of manpower program reform he proposed."[10]

The full Education and Labor Committee was scheduled to meet at 10 A.M. the morning following the all-night marathon bargaining session. No one outside of O'Hara, Steiger, and the staff peo-

---

[8] Ibid., pp. 14–15.
[9] Ibid., p. 18.
[10] James D. Hodgson to Carl D. Perkins (September 30, 1970).

ple had seen the finished product.[11] Yet Democrats, upon arriving at the committee meeting, were greeted by labor and urban lobbyists, who urged them to support the substitute bill. Meanwhile, Republicans were informed that the administration was behind the measure.

Once a quorum was finally obtained, Daniels explained that the meeting had been called to consider H.R.19377, which his subcommittee had ordered reported the day before. However, he yielded to O'Hara to explain the new bill, an "amendment in the nature of a substitute." O'Hara reminded the members of the 25 days of hearings that had been held, described the all-night meeting, and praised the diligence of all of the negotiators. Steiger and Quie supported O'Hara's remarks and indicated their support. Then O'Hara and Steiger undertook to explain the new bill, confessing that it was "mostly a clip and paste job"—an obvious fact, since the members had before them photostatic copies of the handiwork. But they assured their colleagues that the substitute embodied language from several previously introduced measures. Committee members launched into a lengthy dispute over committee and House rules, with Roman Pucinski (D-Ill.) leading the opposition to taking up a bill substantially different than the one advertised.

When bells sounded to signal the start of the House floor session, Chairman Perkins adjourned the meeting in confusion. Several members were seeking to be recognized and shouting their opposition to the parliamentary procedure that had been followed in the meeting. Daniels' motion to adopt H.R.19377, as amended, had been approved by a 23 to 6 vote; but it appeared that supporters of the new bill had neglected to ask for a vote on the

[11] Committee Chairman Perkins and subcommittee Chairman Daniels, preoccupied with occupational safety legislation and not themselves manpower experts, delegated their interests to O'Hara and the committee staff. The committee's ranking Republican, William Ayres (Ohio), was not personally interested and designated Steiger to uphold the minority's interests—though Quie, as senior GOP manpower spokesman, was present for part of the negotiations. Treatment of the manpower bill was a superb illustration of specialization in the House.

substitute itself—that is, H.R.19519. Lacking House approval for meeting during the floor session, the committee had to adjourn with the question unresolved. Thus it happened that a second committee meeting was held later that day. The parliamentary situation was finally unravelled, and the substitute bill placed before the members. Virtually the only committee discussion of the substantive provisions of the measure took place during the next half hour. Representative Edith Green (D-Ore.) posed a series of questions and two minor amendments were agreed to. Finally, H.R.19377 was reported out by a vote of 25 to 3, with Mrs. Green voting "present."[12]

Despite the wrangling over procedures, the deliberations on the compromise bill were unusually brief for the conflict-ridden Education and Labor Committee. However, it illustrates how well-oiled the legislative process can appear when acknowledged experts in a particular field get together. As one political observer explained, with the committee's experts and the administration in agreement, "clearly the fix was on." As long as the Democratic and Republican manpower experts supported the bill, and as long as the administration, labor, and urban interests backed them up, there was little the other committee members could do. In fact, not one of them had a precise idea what was in the photostatic copies of the amalgam measure placed before them. The failure to involve these legislators in the bargaining process was later to have unfortunate consequences, as opposition to H.R.19519 broke out among committee members both on the House floor and in the House–Senate conference.

HOUSE PASSAGE

Parliamentary procedure requires time and meticulous care whenever controversial matters are involved. The roadblocks to

[12] Voting against the bill were three conservatives—William Scherle (Iowa), James Collins (Tex.), and Earl Landgrebe (Ind.). Records of the Committee and Subcommittee sessions are found in the files of the Education and Labor Committee.

obtaining legislative action are especially formidable when, as in the case of H.R.19519, a measure does not emerge from committee until late in the legislative session. Even though the 1970 session had dragged on, Congress was far from completing its agenda. In order to give impatient legislators an opportunity to campaign for reelection, leaders of both parties had agreed to schedule a recess for the election. Late in November, the legislators would return for a "lame-duck session."

The Rules Committee did not get around to discussing the manpower bill until the afternoon before the final day of the regular session. Before reaching the House floor, important bills reported by a substantive committee must be granted a "rule" which specifies the terms of the floor deliberations—the amount of time to be allotted for the debate, whether the bill will be open to floor amendments, and whether points of order will be recognized against certain portions of the bill. The House Committee on Rules, which grants these rules, is an autonomous and conservative body of 15 men. Not only does it serve a "traffic cop" function in granting rules, but it sometimes assumes for itself the responsibility of passing on the substantive merits of legislation.[13] Like many measures emanating from the Education and Labor Committee, therefore, the manpower bill was received with poorly-veiled hostility. The chairman, William Colmer (D-Miss.), at one point asked Steiger whether it was not true that governors were opposed to the bill. The National Governors' Conference, Steiger replied, had no official position, but as far as he knew his own governor would favor it. Later O'Hara was able to produce a telegram (procured by the Labor Department) from Michigan's Governor William Milliken, a Republican, praising the bill and urging its passage. In the end, the Rules Committee granted the manpower bill the requested two-hour open rule.[14]

The following day—the last before the election recess—the Comprehensive Manpower Act became pending business on the

[13] See James Robinson, *The House Committee on Rules* (Indianapolis: Bobbs-Merrill, 1963).

[14] H. Res. 1252, 91st Cong., 2nd sess., 1970.

House floor. Although the House rules prohibit filibusters, energetic legislators have at their disposal several delaying tactics, such as insisting on quorum calls and demanding roll-call votes. Usually these tactics have little more than a nuisance value; but on the final day of a session, with members impatient to leave Washington and begin their campaigning, there was no way to keep the floor business going. Three legislators (including Mrs. Green) were the first to raise points of no quorum; and though quorums were finally obtained in each case, about a dozen members were on the floor and ready to interpose delaying tactics for the remainder of the day. There was nothing to do but adjourn.

The delaying tactics confirmed the presence of more than token resistance to the manpower proposal. A portion of the opposition came from conservatives who were adamant against direct governmental subsidies for jobs, as embodied in the public-service title. More worrisome was the variety of complaints being heard from vocational educators, employment service officials, a few governors, and a few local labor councils. Vocational educators and employment service officials had reason to be dissatisfied that the bill seemingly bypassed them; but lack of time had prevented their interest groups from mobilizing their forces. Others were concerned because the bill guaranteed a linkage between manpower programs and community action agencies. These individuals contacted friendly legislators to enlist their help in delaying H.R.19519.

The Labor Department's legislative liaison staff spent much of their time during the congressional recess trying to broaden the bill's support, or at least neutralize possible opposition. Lovell and his aides met with leaders from the Interstate Conference of Employment Security Agencies to explain the provisions of the bill. The employment security officials were jittery because the proposed act contained virtually no mention of their organizations; in response, the departmental spokesmen pointed to similar omissions in MDTA and EOA. As one of the administration officials explained,

These Acts specify practically no role for the ES agencies, and yet here they are in fact playing a major role in the delivery of services under each of them. So it's a matter of getting the ES people not to be too suspicious of legislative provisions, which are framed in rather general words. Out in the field, these ES people tend to read the most drastic and negative things into legislative provisions.

ICESA's Executive Committee drafted several proposed amendments, but the organization decided not to oppose the Comprehensive Manpower Act. However, individual employment service officials in several states continued to lobby against H.R.19519.

In a similar position were the vocational educators, many of whom feared that the manpower legislation would foster a dual school system to rival their own established system of training. Trying to neutralize possible opposition, Lovell met with Lowell Burkett, director of the American Vocational Association; and, like the ICESA, the AVA decided not to oppose the bill as an organization. An exchange of letters, however, produced assurances of Lovell's commitment to "the fullest utilization of the educational system under this bill . . ."; HEW Secretary Elliott Richardson declared that the bill would "assist the department to make vocational education more effective in meeting the manpower needs of our nation," and that the dual school system argument was "without foundation."[15]

The efforts to defeat H.R.19519 were fueled by Representative Green (D-Ore.), who voiced most of the major objections being raised about the compromise proposal. She was incensed by the Labor Department's seeming incursion into the prerogatives of the educational establishment—that is, the vocational educators. Further, although not opposed to public-service employment, Mrs. Green wanted a provision that would help relieve the high costs of welfare outlays and unemployment insurance. In addition, she was extremely unhappy about the large emphasis placed on community action agencies in the compromise bill. As author of a 1967 amendment to the Economic Opportunity Act designed to strengthen the control exercised by general governments, Mrs. Green had long warred against the CAA's.

[15] The exchange of letters is reprinted in *Congressional Record*, daily ed., November 17, 1970, pp. H10366–69.

During the election recess, Mrs. Green and her administrative assistant, Richard Feeney, busied themselves mobilizing opposition to the Comprehensive Manpower Act. They were able to fan a few fires of concern—especially in Oregon and neighboring states—but they found most of the national lobbies had already closed their doors upon opposition to the bill. As Feeney recalled, "We were getting shut out all the way around." Still Edith Green's office served as a clearinghouse for the various factions working in uncoordinated fashion against the measure.

Debate on the Comprehensive Manpower Act took place on the second day of the lame-duck session. With backing from liberals and the Nixon forces, it passed the House easily—though a segment of hard-core opposition was in evidence.

While the opposition made little headway, it produced some lively rhetoric. The subcommittee's ranking Republican, William Scherle (Iowa), declared that he was disappointed with his GOP colleagues because "this is not a compromise bill at all. It was a Potsdam agreement."[16] He wondered out loud why the administration had abandoned President Nixon's original proposal. The answer probably lay, he said, in the fact that "this bill could be written in a single sentence: 'The Department of Labor is hereby authorized to spend $7.5 billion for whatever manpower training programs it wishes to conduct in any manner it sees fit.'" Meanwhile, Mrs. Green's almost single-minded antipathy toward the community action agencies found many sympathizers among conservative legislators. She charged that H.R.19519

. . . puts the community action agencies in charge of manpower programs—if city mayors do not want to be prime sponsors. Although an effort appears in the bill to involve "local units of government," this is deceptive, for community action agencies retain the major role . . . an expanded role for CAA's that have not been outstanding by past performances.[17]

In contrast to this alleged emphasis on CAA's, Mrs. Green portrayed the bill as diminishing the authority of state and local

[16] *Congressional Record*, daily ed., November 17, 1970, p. H10380.
[17] Ibid., p. H10385.

agencies—including vocational education, employment service, governors, and mayors.

The bill's managers attempted to counter these arguments by pointing to the required integration of manpower programs and to the letters of support from various officials. Finally, however, Steiger became exasperated at Mrs. Green's repeated criticisms and was led to declare:

I believe it also ought to be clear for those who say there is an effort to create a dual school system, that simply does not stand up under the light of examination. With all due respect to the gentlewoman from Oregon, I simply do not understand why she has gone as far as she has in attempting to make the statement that there was any kind of effort to create a dual school system.

He denied Mrs. Green's contention that the school systems ever had been primarily involved in manpower training, and pointed to the bill as a significant step in placing ultimate responsibility in the elected public officials. "There is not an expanded role for the community action agencies," Steiger was led to retort. "If anything, we bring the community action agency more into the mainstream of the agencies serving the public than they have been in the past. . . ."[18]

In view of the curious committee history of the measure, it was not surprising that opponents referred caustically to the "round-the-clock private negotiations" which had produced the bill. Mrs. Green, for example, supplied an interesting commentary on the bipartisan compromise:

. . . This was a bill literally put together in the middle of the night, and finished at 3:30 in the morning by two or three Members and staff people. There were parts and pieces and bits of six or seven different manpower training programs put in this new 72-page bill. No one except the two or three of the 35 Members [of the Committee] knew which parts of which bills were retained or which parts of which bills were dropped. On that same day at 10:30, the meeting was called, and there was no one except the two or three Members who worked on that full Committee who had an opportunity even to read the bill to find out what was in it. The 72-page bill, with some new material

[18] Ibid., p. H10398.

5

The Coalition Comes Apart

Manpower legislation now traveled to a new arena, the conference committee created to resolve differences between S.3867 and H.R.19519. Compared to floor or committee politics, House-Senate conferences receive almost no attention from the world outside Capitol Hill. Most people assume that a bill has been "passed" once it is voted by the two houses, forgetting that conferences represent a kind of third chamber. Proceedings for these ad hoc committees are secret, few records are kept, and public rhetoric after the fact is rarely designed to illuminate. In the case of the 1970 manpower legislation, the conference marked a break-up of the bipartisan coalition which had stood behind manpower training legislation for almost a decade.

THE CONFERENCE COMMITTEE'S REPORT

The final legislation would, of course, fall somewhere between Nelson's S.3867 and the House compromise version, H.R.19519. Yet at least one set of bargainers, the Labor Department managers, had already searched their souls in reaching the House compromise; whether they could concede much more ground remained to be seen. They therefore lost no time in preparing for the conference. As the conferees met, a letter signed by Secretary Hodgson was sent to all the conferees. The statement reminded the legislators that the administration's support of manpower legislation was "predicated on the acceptance of certain basic concepts embodied in the House bill." Six features were cited as "essential": (a) Public-service employment "must provide a transition to nonsubsidized public and private employment for a majority of participants . . . while creating additional permanent public-service jobs." Cited at this point was Section 102(h) of the House bill, which required prime sponsors to set objectives for moving public-service employees into nonsubsidized jobs. (b) Required funding levels for public-service employment "should not exceed that which can be accommodated within realistic budget constraints and current program commitments." (c) Manpower funds must be apportioned "in a flexible fashion at the state and local level to permit comprehensive programs designed to meet each community's needs." (d) A "meaningful state planning role" must permit the states to mesh their resources with local plans. (e) "Effective decategorization" of manpower program authorizations must be achieved. (f) The law "must not be so administratively complex as to invite inefficiency and duplication of activities." The secretary concluded that it was "vital" that these principles be maintained in the conference bill.[1]

The conferees met during the first week of December, with Senator Nelson presiding.[2] In the expanded group, the chief negotiators tended to be the same as they had been in the respective committees: Nelson and Javits from the Senate, and O'Hara, Quie, and Steiger from the House. Staff members participated in the negotiations, especially on behalf of senators; House conferees, in contrast, usually negotiated on their own behalf. House Republicans were usually out in force; but the only Senate GOP

---

[1] James D. Hodgson to conferees, December 7, 1970.

[2] According to conference practice, Nelson and Perkins chaired their respective delegations, each of which would decide by majority vote how to cast their single bloc vote on questions to be resolved. Thus, on contested matters, one of the delegations must "recede," or an acceptable compromise must be found.

spokesman was Javits, and he could not be present for every session. Once more the administration was encountering trouble finding a Senate spokesman.

Among the many issues to be resolved by the conference were four whose resolution would determine the success or failure of the negotiations. These issues were: (1) the definition of local prime sponsors; (2) the role of the states; (3) the issue of categorical programs; and (4) the type and scope of the public-service jobs program. The last issue was by far the most delicate.

The entire prime sponsorship issue took no more than 30 minutes of the conferees' time, and the compromise was, one observer put it, "surprisingly easy." The conferees decided to accept the House figure of 100,000 as the minimum population base for counties or combinations of local governments; the Senate figure of 75,000 was retained for cities. A compromise also emerged on the role of the states, though the bargaining was somewhat more difficult. The Senate conferees were "absolutely paranoid" (as one representative phrased it) about avoiding the slightest hint of a state veto over local manpower planning. The final bargain preserved the concept of the state plan, as well as the linkage between the employment service and the newer manpower programs. A limited right of appeal for local governments was preserved, though all mention of community action agencies was deleted.

Almost everyone conceded that most of the categorical programs of the Senate bill would survive, and indeed the conference bill represented a triumph for the Senate position. "I don't like it at all," said one GOP representative. "Not only did the categorical programs survive the conference; but they were actually increased." The conference bill seemed as inflexible as S.3867 in tying funds to various special programs; and Indians, non-English-speaking people, and migrant workers would receive a proportion of total manpower funds equal to their share of the low income population. However, the administration's "sleeper" amendment remained a part of the bill, and the secretary was further authorized to transfer up to 25 percent of the categorical funds among categories.

58

Neither the House conferees nor administration officials were happy with the categorization, but the senators were adamant that categorical funding be maintained. Lacking the broad intellectual commitment to manpower policy that marked the thinking of such representatives as O'Hara, Steiger, or Quie, the senators manifested their support mainly in terms of specific programs. And several House Democrats joined the senators in arguing for special programs for migrants, Indians, and Spanish-speaking people. O'Hara and the House Republicans were simply outflanked.

The ideological and practical issues surrounding public-service employment divided the conferees most sharply and eventually served to disintegrate the bipartisan coalition. The Administration and those House Republicans who supported H.R.19519 were willing to accept public-service jobs only if they were understood to be short-term jobs—stopgap employment for periods of time when individuals cannot find employment in other public or private jobs. To uphold this principle, the Labor Department insisted on being granted an unambiguous mandate from Congress to enforce the concept. The department was protected in the House compromise bill by provisions which required the local sponsor to set objectives for the movement of persons into non-subsidized jobs. If these objectives were not being achieved, the secretary was required to reduce the federal share of the program's cost.

Nelson and his colleagues were not about to allow the Labor Department those protections. "We didn't trust the Secretary of Labor to run the public-service employment part of the bill," said a Senate aide. The "negotiated objectives" language, they feared, would permit the department to talk communities out of a meaningful public-service program by asking them to attain unreasonable goals. Nor did Nelson wish to grant the secretary power to reduce the federal share of program costs. It would inevitably cause problems for the mayors, who might encounter political resistance to phasing out subsidized jobs once they had been established. It would further mean the closing down of public-service programs, since mayors would not be able to produce more than the basic 20 percent contribution. These arguments confirmed the House Republicans' fears that a massive, permanent program would result. Nelson used the phrase "employer of first resort" rather than "employer of last resort" to characterize his position, which he explained repeatedly. He was able to call on Javits to support him on this and other key issues.

Needless to say, the conference report reflected essentially the Senate's position on public-service employment. The final bill provided for an annual review of the status of each person employed in a subsidized job. If there were insufficient prospects for advancement or suitable continued employment, the trainee would be assisted in securing another job or training spot. The final provisions were agreed upon after a frantic weekend of drafting last minute compromise proposals. The crucial vote in the conference came on a motion that the House conferees "recede" from H.R.19519 and accept essentially the Senate provision controlling public-service employment. It was a straight party vote with the Republicans in the minority. According to the practice of conference committees, the House conferees then cast a single bloc vote to accept the Senate position. At this point Quie and Steiger announced they would not be able to sign the conference report.

The next day, at the instigation of Chairman Perkins, the conference briefly reconvened so that the public-service funding totals could be pared down, a last minute attempt to avert the threat of a veto by President Nixon. But the change was mainly a cosmetic one.

In the aftermath of the House-Senate conference, House Republicans accused Democratic House conferees of yielding too quickly to the Senate's position. "It was not a compromise," a Republican staff aide said, "it was a sell-out." Most Republicans agreed that O'Hara, the chief House negotiator, at least appeared to be fighting valiantly to retain the House position. All of them agreed that other House Democrats—philosophically more attuned to the Senate bill than to the House compromise—"capitulated right off the bat" in urging the House conferees to "recede" from critical provisions of H.R.19519. Republicans based their complaints on the theory that conferees are duty bound to reflect the position embodied in the bill as passed by their house.[3] Democratic conferees countered that they were not bound to vote down the line for the House public-service employment provisions. They accused the Labor Department of insisting on language "which would allow them to put the blame on Congress if money were not available to the various states and localities." O'Hara, for his part, believed that the Labor Department had shifted its ground and thrown up new barriers to a compromise. In the wake of the charges exchanged among disgruntled conferees, it must be concluded that the liberal coloration of the House Democratic contingent and the Nelson-Javits alliance in the Senate were probably the basic causes of the administration's distress.

The conference report on S.3867, now styled as the "Employment and Manpower Act" (or EMA), was taken almost immediately to the Senate floor, where it was promptly passed. Javits characterized the bill as "the very best that can be done." "I hope very much the Senate will adopt it," he said, "and I hope very much the president will sign it into law."[4] Not to be outdone, Nelson declared that the Employment and Manpower Act "would bring the new federalism at its finest to the manpower programs." Both men stressed compromises on funding levels and various other features of the bill, and underscored the safeguards in the public-service jobs section. As Javits explained,

I think we wrestled through the situation, and now have a technique by which there will be a real impetus toward a movement of people who are on public service jobs from those jobs to normal public and private employment, through reevaluation of their talents and maximum efforts to place them.[5]

[3] Conduct of Education and Labor Committee's conferees was discussed during debate over the conference report on the Occupational Health and Safety Act of 1970—in which a manpower conference was frequently mentioned. See *Congressional Record*, daily ed., December 17, 1970, pp. H11892–901.

[4] Senate consideration of the conference report is recorded in *Congressional Record*, daily ed., December 9–10, 1970, pp. S19852–77 and S19952–59.

[5] Ibid., p. S19874.

The letter urged the president to sign the bill as a way of allowing local institutions to plan job creation "to match people who need jobs with useful public service jobs that are badly needed."[8] Various claims made for the act implied that virtually all of the money would go directly into job creation. Such appeals, designed to maximize the public attractiveness of the bill, also served to put White House staff people on their guard. It only confirmed their fears that the bill would constitute an entering wedge for a massive new cadre of public jobholders.

Just as the bill was cleared by both houses, and rumors were circulating about a possible presidential veto, it so happened that the National League of Cities was holding its annual convention in Atlanta. The Executive Committee of the League, which has a strong base in smaller communities, quickly adopted a strong statement urging the President to sign the conference bill. A number of the mayors of the largest cities deputized John Gunther, executive director of the U.S. Conference of Mayors, to return to Washington to lobby for the bill and arrange for the mayors of the "big ten" cities to have an audience with the president. The mayors were not able to gain an appointment to see the president—a tip-off that a veto was forthcoming.

Forces favorable to the legislation were not the only ones trying to gain the ear of the president. The House Republican conferees urged the White House and the Labor Department to veto the measure. As one of the conferees said, the feeling was "strong on our side" that the president ought to veto the bill. In fact, the major fear among House Republicans was that the president might be intimidated by the bill's attractiveness and sign it into law.

Members of the Labor Department staff were working frantically to prepare materials for a recommendation to the White House. Several summaries of the bill's provisions were drawn up, focusing on the problems from the administration's viewpoint. The staff found several ways in which they could have implemented the Employment and Manpower Act according to their own objectives.

[8] Peter Braestrup, "Manpower Bill Backed by Gardner," *Washington Post*, December 17, 1970, p. G–7.

"We could have overcome some of the rigidities of categorical funding," one aide said, "by stretching the wording, and even perhaps going beyond congressional intent." In other areas, however, it would be more hazardous to twist the language of the Act.

Labor Department policymakers claimed they fully expected their recommendation, whether favorable or unfavorable, to be accepted by the White House. However, it was not lost on these same individuals that George Shultz, an advocate of the original Manpower Training Act in 1969 and now a top White House advisor as OMB Director, was not at all happy with the piece of legislation which Congress had returned for the president's signature. As for the public-service jobs notion, he had proved more consistently hostile than his successor. The year before, in hearings on FAP, Shultz had explained to the House Ways and Means Committee his views on the concept:

It is not our intent to create jobs in the public sector especially for the hard-core unemployed as a way of solving manpower problems. We believe that such jobs are not a solution to employment problems, and represent instead a failure to face up to the more difficult task of equipping individuals to compete for the ever-increasing number of real jobs that our economy is producing. . . . Government should assume a responsibility for maintaining a healthy economy that produces enough jobs, and commit itself to preparing people to fill these jobs. We want no work-inventing system that offers a way around this basic responsibility.[9]

The veto of the Employment and Manpower Act came in a message released by the White House on the evening of December 16, 1970. In the message, the president charged that the Employment and Manpower Act "only perpetuates and extends the deficiencies in our manpower programs."[10] In the style of such documents, the message painted the conference bill in harsh language. The public-service jobs provision came in for the

[9] U.S. House of Representatives, Committee on Ways and Means, *Hearings on Social Security and Welfare Proposals*, 91st Cong., 1st sess., 1969, pp. 267–68.

[10] President's veto message on the Employment and Manpower Act, December 16, 1970.

toughest criticism. While conceding that the administration supported "transitional and short-term" public-service employment (as specified in the House bill) as a "useful component" of the nation's manpower policies, the president criticized the conference bill as representing "dead-end jobs in the public sector."

WPA-type jobs are not the answer for the men and women who have them, for government which is less efficient as a result, or for the taxpayers who must foot the bill.

The other unacceptable feature cited in the president's message was decategorization. Claiming that the conference bill would expand the number of program categories, the president said that such provisions would "hamstring the efforts of communities to adjust to change in their local needs." The president pledged to work for an acceptable manpower reform proposal, and invited Congress to act on his other new federalism programs.

A veto message is hardly a measuring rod upon which incumbent Presidents should be judged. Its purpose is to persuade the public of the rightness of the president's actions, and the calamitous consequences of signing the measure before him. Thus, the bleakest interpretation is placed on a piece of legislation which is in all probability the compromise product of many minds. Such was the case in this veto message: it is useful mainly because it identified the reasons for the president's veto. As an analysis of the bill before the president, the message had little to commend it. The reference to "WPA-type jobs" was especially questionable and provoked dismay, not only among friends of the bill but in the Labor Department as well; but interestingly enough, it was this single reference which made the message most effective—since no one is in favor of make-work jobs. Many legislators, not knowing what was in the bill, were frightened off by that phrase alone.

The veto was not popular. To be sure, the wrath of the bill's supporters could be anticipated. John Gunther of the U.S. Conference of Mayors immediately reported that the mayors were "horrified" at the veto. "It is inconceivable," he said,

that the President himself has vetoed the first major legislation reflecting his own concept of the new federalism . . . without even so much as consulting with the mayors who are so closely and immediately affected.[11]

Gunther noted that 15 large-city mayors had been trying to meet with the president for several days and had been "continually turned away."

The liberal press was quick to fault President Nixon for the veto. The *Washington Post* termed it a "strange veto" and contested the president's contentions that the bill would perpetuate categorical programs and foster "WPA-type jobs." Its editorial writers wondered why the bill could be criticized for categorization when it would reduce from 10,000 to an estimated 400 the number of local sponsors of manpower programs. They further noted that in the public-service jobs provision "Congress built in substantial safeguards against any reversion to WPA days." "Some of the language in the veto message," they concluded, "raises a serious question as to whether the President fully understands what Congress was trying to do."[12] The *New York Times* also found the veto hard to understand. "As almost any mayor could tell the President," the writers declared,

there is no alternative to federally financed public service jobs to meet the double crunch of rising unemployment and unbalanced municipal budgets. It is difficult to reconcile Mr. Nixon's veto attack on dead-end WPA-type jobs with his solicitude for the survival of financially shaky aerospace companies. Apparently, one man's Lockheed is another man's leaf-raking.[13]

The Republican *Washington Evening Star* was no happier with the veto—which its writers thought "showed insufficient concern for the nation's unemployed, many of whom owe their idle status to Mr. Nixon's past efforts to fight inflation."[14]

On Capitol Hill, the veto intensified the bad blood between congressional Democrats and the administration on manpower

[11] Carroll Kilpatrick, "Nixon Vetoes Public Jobs Training Bill," *Washington Post*, December 17, 1970, p. A–14.

[12] Editorial, "Strange Veto of the Manpower Bill," *Washington Post*, December 18, 1970, p. A–26.

[13] Editorial, "The Lively Duck," *New York Times*, December 24, 1970.

[14] Editorial, "Duty to the Jobless," *The Washington Evening Star*, December 9, 1970, p. A–10.

issues. O'Hara in particular was angered at what he called "bad faith" in the veto of the bill. Publicly, he charged that the administration had been opposed all along to the public-service section, merely seizing on minor differences over the conference report as an excuse to veto it. He noted that the administration had fought the notion until shortly before the November elections; when they found it "expedient" in a time of rising unemployment to endorse the concept. After the election was over, they found reasons to back down from their position. Probably closer to O'Hara's real belief was the charge that the administration's opposition was mainly the result of nit-picking on the part of "ideologues" in the Labor Department. On the House floor, he heatedly denounced the reservations of administration officials concerning public-service jobs.

If Messrs. Nixon, Shultz, and Hodgson, and their immediate advisers, are convinced that such jobs are bad for the character, why do they not resign in the morning, and see how morally improving it is for them to try and find new jobs in the employment market we enjoy at this stage of the Nixon game plan?[15]

As principal author of S.3867, Nelson was no more charitable in his assessment of the veto. He too contended that Lovell and his aides had hardened their position on the eve of the House–Senate conference, perhaps as the result of pressure from the White House. It was the administration, Nelson contended, that had initially tried to create second class public jobs, by suggesting that federally subsidized wages be held to 80 percent of prevailing wages and by seeking to limit the period of employment to two years or less. And it was the administration that had confused its own position by abandoning these earlier efforts in H.R.19519 by asking simply for greater controls and "objectives."[16]

A presidential veto is sent to the house which originated the measure—in this case the Senate. Initially, Nelson and his staff

[15] *Congressional Record*, daily ed., December 16, 1970, p. H12032. O'Hara entitled his remarks, "And a Merry Christmas to You, Mr. President."
[16] Peter Braestrup, "Little Hope Seen for Manpower Bill in '71," *Washington Post*, January 4, 1971, p. A–2.

people were inclined to avoid a vote on overriding the veto. Even if the two-thirds vote could be mustered in the Senate, the narrowness of the House vote on the conference report indicated the ultimate futility of the action. Moreover, if the Senate were able to override and the House failed to do so by a larger margin than before, would this constitute a further setback for manpower legislation? Nonetheless, the interest groups which had become committed to the act were urging Nelson to schedule a vote; and the seeming unpopularity of the veto gave Nelson and his staff a somewhat inflated sense of optimism. Finally, after consulting with Majority Leader Mike Mansfield (Mont.) and Majority Whip Edward Kennedy (Mass.), Nelson decided to go ahead with the vote. Rather than waiting for further reactions to the veto to set in, the vote would be scheduled as quickly as possible. "We became a little overconfident," subcommittee staff director William Bechtel said. "And we didn't start counting until quite late; the top-heavy Senate vote on the conference report gave us a false sense of security, and we didn't realize how many moderate Republicans we were going to lose."

The Senate floor debate on the president's veto occurred on the evening of December 21, two days before the Christmas adjournment. The debate was relatively uneventful. Since Dominick was still vacationing, Murphy led off for the pro-veto forces and said that although he had voted for the conference report, he now supported the president's veto. Javits announced that he would vote to override the veto. Contending that the veto was probably made solely because of the public-service jobs provision, he disputed the president's contention that the money would turn into dead-end jobs. After a parade of senators placed themselves on the record either for or against the legislation, Nelson summed up the arguments for the legislation. "The veto message which was prepared for the President," he said, "does not accurately reflect the provisions of the bill and in fact is refuted by the specific language of the Act."[17]

[17] The debate is found in *Congressional Record*, daily ed., December 21, 1970, pp. S20966–91.

The vote was 48 to 35 to override the veto. This was a majority, but short of the two-thirds which were needed. In addition to Javits, eight other Republicans voted against the president. Because of the veto, 16 other Republican senators who had earlier voted for the conference report, now voted against the bill. There were also several new negative votes from the Democratic side of the aisle. Thus the original margin in favor of S.3867 was drastically reduced. The presidential veto had been sustained, and the House would not consider the measure again.

Conclusions: "We Came So Close"

The president's veto of the Employment and Manpower Act marked the end of two years of relatively intense attention to the problems of manpower needs and manpower reform. It marked the first time that Congress had given explicit attention to the delivery of manpower services, as opposed to the substance of programs. The significance of the legislative action extended much farther than the particular policy area being discussed. The issues of administrative and federal relationships were symptomatic of the complaints many people were raising about governmental programs in the 1960s and 1970s; and the very issues which were opened by the congressional debates were harbingers of future debates which will strike at the very heart of contemporary politico-administrative problems.

In terms of the history of manpower programs themselves, the events of 1969–1970 represented the first overall assessment of the programs which had proliferated in the 1960s, and the first attempt at major institutional change since MDTA in 1962 and EOA in 1964. Many core issues had been exposed, few had been resolved; and the final legislation was an instructive indicator of the political forces at work. No one achieved what they wanted, but change was definitely in the air. Given the potential influence of such old-line deliverers of service as the vocational educators and the employment security agencies, however, it was uncertain how long a strategy of reform based essentially on bypassing these interests could successfully be pursued.

But it was not these issues, thorny as they were, that shattered the cozy manpower coalition of the 1960s. Rather, the consensus was shattered by ideological divisions which harked back to the very beginning of the modern era of governmental involvement in the economy, dating from the Depression days. Public-service employment—whether one thought of it as new opportunity or as "WPA-type jobs"—was a symbol to which people reacted quite apart from the details of the situation. It was the kind of issue which had divided Democrats and Republicans, liberals and conservatives, for more than a generation; and although such issues were thought to be fading from the scene, it was revived by a period of high unemployment.

For the time being, this ideological issue seemed to scuttle hopes for basic reform of manpower services. Congressional Democrats (not to mention liberal interest groups) were more interested in public-service jobs than in basic manpower reform, and the reform package in H.R.19519 had been possible only as part of a compromise between congressional Democrats and the administration. At best, the bargaining had been hampered by the distrust of such administration actions as the closing of Job Corps centers, the new CEP guidelines, the Labor Department's failure to implement Title I-B of the 1967 EOA amendments, and the seeming downgrading of the Office of Economic Opportunity. To these sources of tension was now added the widespread belief among Capitol Hill Democrats that the Labor Department had been playing games with public-service jobs.

On both sides of Capitol Hill, Democrats appeared to push emergency legislation designed to provide public jobs, with no provision for reform of manpower services. "We are going to bring the job issue before the President in very stark terms," O'Hara was quoted as saying, "so there will be no place for him to hide if he isn't going to approve the bill."[18]

The administration also had to decide which way to move.

[18] Norman C. Miller, in *Wall Street Journal*, January 18, 1971, p. 1. See also James Welsh, "Two Billion Public Jobs Plan Will Be Pushed by Nelson," *Washington Evening Star*, January 19, 1971, p. A–2.

Rising unemployment and the pressures of legislative bargaining had forced the administration to accept a number of compromises, including some form of public-service employment. Some administration strategists felt the compromises had gone too far, and that the president should not have been placed in a position where he had to veto a measure. On the other hand, the administration seemed irrevocably on record in support of the bipartisan House bill or its equivalent. And more importantly, the president's "game plan" for revitalizing the economy was slow in showing results. The December unemployment rate actually rose from 5.8 to 6.0 percent, the highest level in nine years. This had two consequences for the administration's legislative strategy: it gave more credibility to the activities of congressional Democrats in pressing for a public employment measure; and it served to convince the White House to follow a more expansionist economic course, even if that meant incurring a sizeable budget deficit for fiscal 1972.

On balance, these considerations impelled the administration to continue efforts for manpower reform. Shultz passed the word that a new proposal should be prepared, and by mid-January a Labor Department official promised that "we will definitely go back with a new bill. It will be high-priority legislation."[19] Several alternative approaches were studied by the Labor Department. In the meantime, however, the White House staff became absorbed in a very different strategy for reforming federal programs. This was the notion of revenue-sharing.

[19] James Welsh, "Manpower Bill Readied by Nixon," *Washington Evening Star*, January 14, 1971, p. 2.

6

Ideological Conflicts

If the events of the 91st Congress accurately reflected the disagreements over reforms in federal domestic aid programs, they also left a bitter aftertaste at both ends of Pennsylvania Avenue. Insofar as they talked for the record, administration officials fell into line behind the president's veto; privately, they seemed somewhat chastened by the entire series of events. Nonetheless, the word was passed that the president wanted a new legislative effort to overhaul federal training programs. Capitol Hill Democrats, however, were in no hurry to reopen a bipartisan dialogue on manpower programs. Neither Nelson nor O'Hara, for example, were anxious to renew the complicated deliberations that would be needed to overhaul manpower training programs—even though both conceded the desirability of reform. Public-service jobs were another matter; and with unemployment remaining high, Democrats were rallying around the notion of public-service employment. The lines were soon drawn for a partisan and ideological donnybrook.

The Administration: Moving the Court

At the time he vetoed the Nelson bill, President Nixon had virtually promised to submit a new bill for the 92nd Congress.

Subsequent developments—continuing high unemployment, the stirrings of congressional Democrats, and the emerging "expansionary" budget for fiscal 1972—seemed to reinforce this decision. Early in January, Labor Department drafters began to prepare suggestions for the new bill, all in the framework of the Manpower Training Act or the House-passed compromise.

Meanwhile, at the White House, the Domestic Council staff was casting about for new ideas for the president's second State of the Union address. They decided on a course which would fold the manpower reform efforts into a large-scale program of revenue-sharing: that is, federal funding for other governmental entities with few or no conditions on how the money is to be spent.

In 1969, President Nixon had presented a modest revenue-sharing proposal as part of his new federalism package.[1] The plan would have increased the level of revenue-sharing from $500 million during the first year to $5 billion a year by fiscal 1976. Funds would have been divided among the states according to population and state revenue-raising efforts; cities and counties would receive a portion of their state's share according to their own relative fund raising efforts. The proposal would therefore not only pump additional money into local governments, but would also encourage them to adopt strong tax systems. The president advocated this mechanism to strengthen state and local governments so that "the political landscape of America will be visibly altered, and states and cities will have a far greater share of power and responsibilities for solving their own problems."

The important feature of the president's 1969 plan, like earlier proposals of the mid-1960s, was that the funds were considered a bonus, above and beyond existing federal commitments. Thus, at least in the short run, they would not threaten established grant-in-aid programs and the interests which support them. This theme permeated the 1969 Senate hearings on revenue-sharing, during which Assistant Secretary of the Treasury Murray Weidenbaum

---

[1] The president's bill, described in a message of August 13, 1969, was introduced in Congress as S.2948 and H.R.13982.

(whose staff prepared the president's bill) assured that the proposal was "additive, not substitutive."[2] As for the ultimate objective of reducing categorical programs, Weidenbaum quoted Ibsen's principle of "a discreet moderation and a moderate discretion."

The administration's "discreet" proposal had netted much generalized praise but very little congressional action. Although the prospective beneficiaries were enthusiastic, they did not precipitate much political action. As we have seen lobbyists for the states did not demonstrate an impressive legislative clout. City interests, desperate for new funds and blessed with a large and effective Washington lobby, did not bestir themselves on revenue-sharing because they believed generally that they could obtain more from existing categorical grant programs.[3] In legislative circles, moreover, revenue-sharing was interpreted as a threat to congressional prerogatives. The revenue committees (Ways and Means, Finance) declined to hold hearings; and the open-ended funding feature of the plan raised the ire of the powerful Appropriations Committees, which prefer year by year review of spending.

Revenue-sharing, nonetheless, was not forgotten at the White House when, in the fall of 1970, presidential advisors turned to the task of formulating new proposals for the coming year. Returning from the 1970 campaign convinced that large numbers of citizens felt alienated from government, President Nixon instructed his Domestic Council staff, under the direction of John Ehrlichman, to study a greatly expanded revenue-sharing plan which would shift governmental decisions "closer to the people."[4] Originally discussion centered around proposals for "dissolving specified federal categorical grant programs into a fund suitable for a greatly

[2] U.S. Senate, Committee on Government Operations, Subcommittee on Intergovernmental Relations, *Intergovernmental Revenue Act of 1969 and Related Legislation* (91st Cong., 2nd sess., 1970), pp. 166, 171.

[3] See Arnold Cantor, "Revenue Sharing: Passing the Buck," *The American Federationist* (November 1970), p. 5.

[4] A detailed account of the origins of the president's revenue-sharing proposal appeared in the *National Journal*, 3 (April 3 and 10, 1971): 703–39, 761–807. This account has been used to supplement the author's own interviews and analysis.

expanded program of revenue sharing" (to quote a White House memorandum on the subject). Categorical programs available for such a fund would have totaled more than $15 billion (more than 50 percent of all grant-in-aid funds), including virtually all manpower programs. Pragmatists on Ehrlichman's staff protested that such a course of action would be too extreme and would have little chance of enactment. Thus emerged a modified proposal—comprising a general revenue fund of $5 billion and six "special" funds. At a meeting at Camp David late in December, the various alternatives, ranging from streamlined categorical grant programs to all-out revenue-sharing, were laid before the president. Nixon opted for the modified proposal which included special revenue-sharing. "I've been for bloc-grant programs since the 1950s," he told his advisors. "This time, let's go all the way."

Once the number and scope of the series of special revenue-sharing proposals were decided upon by the White House, responsibility for drafting the legislative proposals was delegated to the agencies involved—to Assistant Secretary Lovell, in the case of manpower. Lovell's staff dusted off their manpower proposals and began to shape them in the form of revenue-sharing. But they soon discovered that revenue-sharing, though aimed at many of the same objectives as prior reform proposals, was quite a different kettle of tea. Rather than retaining strong discretionary authority for the secretary of labor, the revenue-sharing philosophy demanded that the federal government essentially relinquish the manpower business—with the exception of funds retained by the secretary for a few purely national functions.

A brief debate ensued between Hodgson and Lovell on the one hand and the White House negotiators on the other—Shultz, Ehrlichman, and OMB's Richard Nathan. The Labor Department's managers wanted to retain at least 25 percent of the total authorizations, the figure embodied in the 1969 Manpower Training Act. As an alternative, they suggested a graduated apportionment, which would increase the local share over a period of years. White House policymakers insisted on giving 85 percent of the authorizations to state and local governments, with only 15 percent reserved for the department's manpower activities. "Ehrlichman, Shultz, and Nathan were all in there to go pure revenue-sharing, and they prevailed," a Labor Department official reported.

Another critical issue in the negotiations centered around guidelines for spending the money. In the end, the philosophy of revenue-sharing dictated wiping out most of the guidelines. "We decided that if we really mean what we say—that people at the state, county, and local levels are able to determine their own needs—we ought to put our policy where our mouth is and let them decide," Hodgson explained. About the only limitations were those requiring compliance with the 1964 Civil Rights Act and setting a two-year limit on the time an enrollee could remain in a public-service job.

Manpower revenue-sharing emerged as a $2 billion package, of which $1.7 billion would go directly to state and local governments. The remainder would be retained by the secretary for research, demonstration, and technical assistance programs. Money would be distributed to the states and localities according to their percentage of the national total of workers, unemployed persons, and low income people 16 years of age or older. Eligible governments would include states; cities with populations of more than 100,000; counties of the same population; and consortia of local governments representing a total of 75 percent of the population of the area (Standard Metropolitan Statistical Area). No matching funds would be required. Public-service employment would be permitted, so long as the jobs were transitional and aid to a given enrollee did not exceed two years.

On March 4 President Nixon sent Congress a message on manpower revenue-sharing—the second of his special revenue-sharing messages. Reciting all of the faults of categorical programs, the message urged revenue-sharing as a "partnership" that would "make government more responsive to legitimate demands for quality services." The proposal "neither mandates nor terminates any programs." Proven categorical programs would be continued: "Indeed, many current categorical programs probably would continue and expand in response to local needs once arbitrary federal restrictions were removed." On the other hand, ineffective programs which could not meet the marketplace test would be replaced by others.

Vesting the program authority in governments close to the people will make it harder for programs to coast along on their momentum from year to year, and easier to tailor manpower assistance to on-the-scene realities.[5]

Administration publicists tried to sell the new proposal as being very similar to the original Manpower Training Act of 1969. In fact, although both grew out of the same philosophy and were ultimately pointed at the same objectives, there was a fundamental difference. MTA, and for that matter Nelson's S.3867, authorized decentralization of planning and implementing of manpower programs. But at the same time, they envisioned a vigorous role for the federal government in setting and maintaining standards of performance. They were, in a word, consolidated and streamlined federal grant programs. Revenue-sharing, on the other hand, mandated a direct and immediate diminution of federal responsibilities. Beyond the 15 percent of manpower monies to be retained for a few national programs, the Labor Department would have no substantial voice in manpower policies or programs; the money would be handed over to state and local entities, automatically and with few questions asked.

This approach was not destined to be popular in Washington. The agencies which administer programs, not to mention the legislative committees on Capitol Hill which authorize them and the appropriations committees which fund them, do not willingly allow authority to slip through their fingers. In Congress, legislators foster their reputations and careers by remaining alert to local problems and devising or supporting (however desultorily) solutions designed to alleviate them. Even though not experts in manpower programs, most nonetheless assume that their constituents expect them to support various manpower programs and assist in obtaining services for their districts. Nor did the Labor De-

[5] *Congressional Record*, daily ed., March 4, 1971, p. S2401.

partment's managers and technicians embrace the president's proposal with any visible eagerness. Outside of the presidential appointees at the top, who were in any case bound to support the proposal, hardly anyone in the department had much to say about manpower revenue-sharing. After all, officials who are committed to their work (or at least their jobs) are not likely to applaud the dissolution of their agencies.

In any event, no groundswell of legislative support appeared. In the Senate, only four GOP senators were found to co-sponsor S.1234, the manpower revenue-sharing bill.[6] House sponsorship was more impressive: H.R.6181 had ten co-sponsors, including Minority Leader Gerald Ford (Mich.); Quie, the committee's new ranking minority member; Marvin Esch (Mich.), new ranking member on the subcommittee; and Steiger. While outwardly supportive, however, Republican legislators evidenced no great enthusiasm for the proposal.

With the advent of the new White House proposal, an embarrassing hiatus ensued with regard to manpower reorganization. As Secretary Hodgson somewhat apologetically explained to House and Senate committees early in 1971, "I know you think that now that you have come to play ball in our court, we have simply moved the court. To some extent that's true."[7] Few people, it seemed, were ready to play in the administration's new court.

THE DEMOCRATS: RAISING THE STAKES

Unemployment during December 1970 reached 6 percent, the highest figure in nine years. This meant that more than 2 million workers had been thrown out of jobs in the preceding year. It also indicated that the President's "game plan" for revitalizing the economy had yet to produce positive results. Although White House

[6] Javits was noticeably absent from the co-sponsors.

[7] U.S. Senate, Committee on Labor and Public Welfare, Subcommittee on Employment, Manpower, and Poverty, *Emergency Employment Act of 1971*, 92nd Cong., 1st sess., 1971, p. 213. Cited hereinafter as *Senate Hearings*.

economic advisers were continually finding signs that the economy was "turning the corner," it was clear that the corner had not been reached. Many individual communities faced even more serious joblessness, and worried legislators were looking around for solutions. "The whole political climate seemed to change over-night," a Senate aide reported. "We started getting calls from mayors, congressmen, and senators' staffs saying 'you have got to do something.' "[8]

At the same time, increased attention was being devoted to deteriorating public services at the state and local levels. A spate of articles in newspapers and magazines described the impending financial crisis of local and state governments, laying stress on the thousands of unfilled public jobs and the many thousands more that would go unfilled if financial relief were not forthcoming. One AFL-CIO lobbyist related how he became aware of the plight of local governments:

> I met some of the mayors informally. I would be introduced as some-one who helped with the manpower bill. They were talking about the unemployment rate in their cities, the kinds of services they could provide but were having to cut back and lay people off. I knew things were bad, but listening to these guys I got the idea we had to go right away.

Such reports served to convince backers of the unsuccessful Nelson bill to renew their efforts; meanwhile, such groups as Common Cause (which replaced the Urban Coalition Action Council) con-tinued to support public employment to improve local services.

Senator Nelson and his staff were the eager beneficiaries of these forces. As the 92nd Congress convened, the staff produced the "Emergency Employment Act of 1971" (S.31) which would authorize $1 billion to create from 150,000 to 200,000 public-service jobs. S.31 was a categorical program *par excellence*. The secretary of labor was authorized to contract with local sponsors

[8] Charles Culhane, writing in the *National Journal*, 3 (March 27, 1971): 647–56, has provided a relatively accurate account of the events of early 1971. Culhane's account has been utilized to supplement the author's own interviews and examination of the record.

who would create the jobs and provide training for enrollees. Eligible sponsors included states, cities, counties, other units of local government, and public and private institutions, including federal agencies. The federal government would pay 90 percent of the salaries and training for the enrollees, with the local sponsors paying ten percent. Enrollees would receive either the federal minimum wage, the state or local minimum, or the prevailing wage in the area, whichever was higher.

S.31 was shrewdly written, however, so that it would be difficult for the president to use his earlier veto message as a basis for objecting to it. Rather than a permanent program, the new measure was to be operative for a two-year period. Moreover, job creation would be tied to a trigger mechanism: the secretary of labor would be authorized to spend $500 million for public-service jobs when the national rate of employment equaled or exceeded 4.5 percent for three consecutive months. An additional $100 million would be released for each .5 percent increase beyond that figure. Anticipating the criticism of "dead-end jobs," the authors of the new bill required sponsors, where possible, to provide employees with training and place them in jobs with opportunities to advance into nonsubsidized jobs. The secretary was given broad authority to assure that local public-service job programs were: primarily for disadvantaged workers; aimed at satisfying unmet public-service needs; located in expanding occupations which offer advancement; linked to existing or new training and other supportive services; connected to a program of upgrading within the sponsor agency; and subject to periodic reviews of the status of each enrollee.[9]

Nelson and his staff soon discovered they had a popular item on their hands. "The co-sponsors just tumbled in, and the key word was 'temporary,' " Subcommittee Staff Director William Bechtel reported. By the time S.31 was introduced, it had no less than 33 co-sponsors, including the new committee chairman, Harrison A. Williams (D-N.J.), and every major Democratic presidential con-

[9] For Nelson's remarks upon introducing S.31, see *Congressional Record*, daily ed., January 26, 1971, pp. S171–78.

tender in the Senate. The 10 GOP co-sponsors included Javits, as the committee's ranking minority member, along with Minority Leader Hugh Scott (R-Penna.). Javits released a four-page statement explaining his support of the measure, contending it was "in keeping with the philosophy of the Administration." Indeed, the trigger mechanism was almost identical to the one found in the administration's original manpower bill of August 1969—though with almost 10 times the authorization.[10]

Nelson moved quickly to hold hearings on S.31. Appearing on the first day (February 8) were no less than 13 big-city mayors, including chief executives from New York City, Detroit, Philadelphia, and Chicago.[11] "The situation now facing us is no longer isolated and affecting only a few cities," declared Wesley Uhlman of Seattle, where unemployment was 12 percent. "It is a national problem." He and other mayors blamed the increased unemployment on the president's anti-inflation policy. "Unfortunately for many of us, the cure has been worse than the disease," he noted. The mayors stressed that the jobs they had in mind were not makework jobs, but necessary services. Detroit's Democratic mayor, Roman S. Gribbs, said his city had been forced to lay off 600 workers because of a budgetary squeeze. And New York's Mayor John V. Lindsay said the mayors viewed S.31 as an emergency measure, not as a substitute for thoroughgoing manpower reform. "It is an emergency bill for an emergency situation," he said. "We need it because we are in serious trouble."[12] In addition to the mayors, an impressive series of witnesses—including several governors—was easily recruited to speak in behalf of the bill during the four days of hearings.

Labor Secretary Hodgson's appearance before the subcommittee offered an illuminating lesson in legislative-executive relations. Hodgson informed the senators that the administration was against S.31:

[10] Statement of Senator Jacob K. Javits (February 8, 1971).

[11] "Mayors Push City Jobs Plan," *Washington Post*, February 9, 1971, p. A-2.

[12] *Senate Hearings*, pp. 32, 41, 82.

The Administration cannot support a separate public-service employment program which is not an integral part of manpower reform, welfare reform and revenue sharing. We are, in fact, obliged to oppose it.[13]

Hodgson outlined other administration initiatives designed to alleviate unemployment: the expansionary budget, general revenue-sharing, welfare reform, and special revenue-sharing in manpower. All of these, he contended, would produce new public-service jobs.

Hodgson had hardly put down his prepared statement when Nelson launched into a 30-minute lecture on the history of S 3867. Nelson described in great detail the "Herculean effort" which his subcommittee had made to develop an acceptable manpower bill the year before. Even while the president was delivering speeches criticizing Congress for not moving faster on legislation, Nelson said, his subcommittee was laboring diligently to develop a manpower bill with "wide support." After it had passed and rumors of a veto were circulating, Nelson had written to George Shultz asking for an opportunity to argue the case for the bill. "The letter has yet to be answered," Nelson remarked.

I know they're very busy over there [in the White House], but if the President knew what was in the bill, he'd be embarrassed at the words put in his mouth [by the veto message].[14]

Nelson continued that the senators had now given in on every major point made by the administration: local prime sponsors were provided; the program was to be temporary; and there were ample safeguards against dead-end jobs. "Can we put in another ten months on another comprehensive manpower bill?" he queried. "How about good faith? It's very hard to ask this Committee to do another year of work and then perhaps get a veto." Besides, S.31 would deal with "what happens between now and the time the checks can be written" for a comprehensive bill.

Javits joined in warning Hodgson that the administration's new

---

[13] Ibid., p. 212.
[14] Ibid., p. 214.

revenue-sharing proposal would require lengthy examination by Congress. "We are giving you an emergency measure," Javits said.

Your measure is going to take time. It may not even pass in this session of the 92nd Congress. We are offering you some thousands of jobs to try to break this situation, and you say let us take a good long time.[15]

In view of Javits' position, the administration's prospects of convincing the Senate Subcommittee were hopeless.

Hodgson warned that a presidential veto was "a strong possibility" for a bill such as S.31 and pleaded for the senators to wait for the as yet incomplete manpower revenue-sharing bill. To no one's surprise, however, the senators were in no mood to heed Hodgson's admonitions. On March 27, the Nelson-Javits bill breezed through the full Senate Labor and Public Welfare Committee by a vote of 15–2.[16]

Committee Republicans were dispersed by the situation. Three GOP moderates (Javits, plus Richard Schweiker of Pennsylvania and Robert Packwood of Oregon) reserved the right to "seek an accommodation" between S.31 and the president's reform proposal. However, they saw the present legislation as "an acceptable short term and transitional means of alleviating many of the individual hardships imposed by levels of unemployment such as are currently faced."[17] Two others, Winston Prouty (Vt.) and J. Glenn Beall (Md.), reserved the right to offer amendments or even oppose the final measure in light of the revenue-sharing proposal, of which Prouty was chief Senate sponsor. The committee's conservatives, Dominick and Taft, had more substantial objections and voted against the bill.

The progress of S.31 continued unabated when, on April 1, it was considered and approved by the Senate.[18] Only minor changes were made in the committee bill: five amendments passed by voice vote. In a series of roll call votes the Senate rejected, 44–29, a

15 Ibid., pp. 224–25.
16 Senate Rept. 92–48, 92nd Cong., 1st sess., 1971.
17 Ibid., p. 25.
18 *Congressional Record*, daily ed., April 1, 1971, pp. S4306–48.

During debate on the Daniels bill and the Esch substitute, Daniels argued for H.R.3613 as a "modest proposal with a specific, clearly stated purpose." The same measure was labeled by Esch as "an uncoordinated, haphazard, jerry-rigged approach to meeting manpower needs which would put Rube Goldberg to shame."[25]

The GOP-southern victory on the vote over the rule convinced the Democratic leadership to postpone for two weeks the final contest between the two bills. Labor and urban lobbyists swung into action to assure that their friends were solidly behind the public-jobs bill. But the decisive push was made by Speaker Albert and Majority Leader Hale Boggs (La.), who personally made the rounds of southerners' offices to shake loose their support from the Esch substitute. The leaders made it clear that local government officials were solidly behind the public-jobs concept, and that the vote would present a chance to embarrass the Nixon administration. When the crucial votes were finally held on June 2, the leaders' efforts paid off. The Esch substitute was defeated 182–201 on a recorded teller vote. The closest vote came on Esch's motion to recommit H.R.3613, which lost by a 184–202 margin. On both votes, only a handful of Republicans defected to vote for the Daniels bill; but the Democrats were also able to command a strong partisan showing, with no more than a dozen defectors. The Daniels bill was then passed by a 245–141 margin.[26]

The House floor debate yielded a significant colloquy on whether the Esch bill was or was not a revenue-sharing measure.

Quie: The gentleman calls this general revenue sharing . . . but it is instead a consolidation of manpower programs.

· · ·

Perkins: Well, it is the manpower aspects of it.

Quie: He [the president] called it special revenue sharing for manpower for some reason, thinking that that was better than the consolidated manpower program or bloc grants for manpower.

[25] Ibid., pp. H4050, 4053.
[26] Ibid., pp. H4530–39.

Perkins: It is the President's so-called revenue sharing measure that has never been studied by the committee.

Quie: I am glad you called it "so-called."

. . .

Perkins: There is no way for the minority members to get away from the fact that this is a revenue-sharing bill that drastically upsets our educational programs, our manpower programs, and will cause chaos throughout this nation if enacted.

. . .

Steiger: I want to be absolutely clear that the record does not in any way confuse anybody that this is not a new subject, that this is not a new item in the agenda whatsoever, and that what we passed last year had as its basic purpose exactly the kind of bill we are talking about this year.[27]

While these remarks suggested some vagueness surrounding the revenue-sharing concept, they also revealed that the supporters of H.R.8141 were striving to avoid that label. And although legislative bargaining brought the Esch bill close to passage in the House, it was not long before committee Republicans had openly abandoned special revenue-sharing and returned to the approach embodied in the 1970 House compromise.

As the conferees met to reconcile the differences between Nelson's S.31 and Daniels' H.R.3613, the White House decision-makers were forced to reassess the situation. Democratic leaders in both houses had gained impressive support for the public-jobs concept. The conferees would have little trouble reconciling the two bills, and the president would thus confront the unpleasant prospect of vetoing a second such bill in approximately six months. Another Democratic antirecession measure, public works acceleration, had also passed both houses and was on the president's desk. From the White House vantage point, the most salient fact of life was the nine-year unemployment high of 6.2 percent. The president's economic game plan was obviously faltering (and would be abandoned within two months), and some rapid job creation was in order. Besides, the same local officials who were behind revenue-

[27] Ibid., pp. H4052–53.

sharing were also insisting that they needed large numbers of public-service jobs. Moreover, the difficulties encountered by returning Vietnam veterans in finding jobs were gaining wide publicity. A pragmatic approach seemed to be called for.

Faced with a bleak economic picture and an unacceptable public works acceleration bill, the White House decided to veto the public works measure but accept the notion of an emergency, short-term, transitional public-jobs bill. Accordingly, on June 29 the president announced that he was vetoing S.575, which he termed "a poor and distant second" to public-service employment. Earlier, the word had been passed to House and Senate conferees that Nelson's S.31 came closest to the administration's preferences for a law "permitting states and localities to move quickly, and on a sound and responsible basis, to create new job opportunities in the public sector." The message stressed that the Senate bill met the objections of the veto six months earlier:

We have stressed one key point: that these created jobs must be *transitional*—that is, they must be a bridge to permanent, productive jobs, not a substitute for them.

The action taken thus far this year by the Congress on the Emergency Employment Act of 1971 deals effectively with these concerns. Public employment is defined as "transitional." It is targeted on locally-supported jobs of proven need. Moreover, the bill, as it has been agreed to in conference, would be limited to two years and would be triggered when national unemployment exceeds 4.5 percent.[28]

The White House action had consequences for manpower reform. In lending its support to the bill, the administration was able to gain promises that both houses would move rapidly to consider comprehensive manpower legislation, including revenue-sharing.

With the administration's blessing, the conferees quickly reached agreement on the essential provisions of the Senate bill. The veterans' preference feature of the House bill was accepted, however. In reporting the conference bill, the conferees stated that its

[28] Cited in *Congressional Quarterly Weekly Report* 29 (July 16, 1971), p. 1506.

transitional nature was "intended to make it crystal clear that public service employment shall not be of the 'dead end, make work' sort that is feared by the critics."[29] Final approval of the conference report was a simple matter, the Senate voting 75–11 and the House ratifying the action a day later, 343–14.[30] Soon a special appropriation for the program was approved.

The Emergency Employment Act was implemented with what seems to have been remarkable promptness and fairness, considering the multiple bureaucratic levels involved. Of course, such a program was not a panacea for joblessness. The $1 billion initial appropriation was enough for approximately 140,000 positions—only 3 of every 100 unemployed people. However, a preliminary evaluation of the program by Sar A. Levitan concluded that "In terms of reducing unemployment, the Emergency Employment Act was a bargain." It appeared that "a real effort was made to spread jobs equitably among claimant groups"; use of the jobs for political purposes was apparently rare.

For the most part, jobs filled with EEA funds [the evaluation report stated] were vacant because of budget stringencies and in most areas the persons hired included professionals, the unskilled, and the poorly educated. Members of minority groups also got a fair share of the jobs reflecting their high incidence of unemployment.[31]

Most significantly, perhaps, the rapid implementation of EEA seemed to confirm once and for all that thousands of unfilled jobs actually existed at state and local levels, if only the dollars could be found to fill them.

Indeed, the ink was hardly dry on EEA before congressional Democrats began clamoring for greatly expanded public employment funds on a more permanent basis. One of the leading proposals, the so-called "Jobs Now" bill (H.R.12011) introduced by Henry S. Reuss (D-Wis.), would have authorized an expanded EEA to fund an estimated 500,000 jobs. Reuss gathered 62 House

[29] H. Rept., 92–310.
[30] See *Congressional Record*, daily ed., June 29, 1971, p. S10174.
[31] Sar A. Levitan, "Creating Jobs Is One Way to Fight Unemployment," reprinted in *Congressional Record*, daily ed., May 18, 1971, pp. E4546–47.

co-sponsors, while in the Senate it was submitted (as S.3092) by Walter Mondale (D-Minn.) and 21 co-sponsors.[32] Endorsements from leading economists were also obtained. Another proposal, Senator Alan Cranston's (D-Calif.) Public Service Employment Act (S.3311), was a somewhat different and more ambitious program, envisioning no less than $10 billion annually. Other, similar measures were placed into the hopper, and when House and Senate subcommittees got around to holding hearings on manpower reorganization in early 1972, these proposals received prominent attention from witnesses. Clearly, more would be heard concerning public-service employment.

SUMMARY

Delivery of manpower services is a controversial question at best, as the history of recent legislative initiatives shows. The presence of such issues as revenue-sharing and public-service employment raised the level of tension even higher. It was the ideological gulf surrounding public-sector jobs that finally spelled the defeat of legislation in 1970, as we have seen. President Nixon's special revenue-sharing proposal added fuel to the fire because it seemed ill-tailored to congressional prerogatives or to political or administrative experience with manpower programs. These differences, it cannot be forgotten, came to a head during a period of relatively high unemployment.

In the aftermath of President Nixon's 1970 veto, therefore, a highly partisan atmosphere prevailed, with the antagonists determined that their viewpoints should prevail. On Capitol Hill, Democrats talked of pushing through programs which would embarrass the president. On the other end of Pennsylvania Avenue, President Nixon and his advisors took a hard line on congressionally originated categorical programs. Bitterness over the previous year's legislative events suffused the atmosphere.

[32] *Congressional Record*, daily ed., December 2, 1971, p. H11742.

The détente which made possible the Emergency Employment Act temporarily cleared the air. Special revenue-sharing was being allowed to die a quiet death, and legislators from both sides of the aisle maneuvered back toward the compromise of 1970. But the apparent success of EEA, plus unemployment that remained above 5 percent, soon produced new demands for expanded public-service employment. Again manpower reorganization was all but over-shadowed by the promise of new funds which would confirm the government's role as employer of last resort.

Partisan politics, of course, had something to do with these trends. Government in Washington was divided, and 1972 was a presidential election year, and joblessness remained high enough to be irresistible as a political issue. Thus it was not surprising that politicians and interests who had long advocated public-service employment would take advantage of propitious circum-stances to campaign for the concept. As long as such circumstances continued, therefore, it seemed that manpower reform legislation would have to be coupled with an attractive job-creation program. The necessities of politics would at least point definitely in the direction of such a compromise as the *quid pro quo* whereby reorganization could be pushed through Congress.

These considerations are above all political, but they are not wholly partisan. Like most matters dealing with structures and procedures, manpower reorganization lacks broad political appeal. It is not surprising that manpower reorganization has been pushed most enthusiastically by high-level administrators, academicians, and technical experts with a commitment to the manpower field. A number of politicians who deal with the subject have been persuaded of the need for such reorganization, but it seems to hold less appeal for them than does the substance of manpower pro-grams. In contrast to procedural issues, the bread-and-butter issues of federal services, and the dollars that go with them, are easily assimilated and dealt with by elective officials. Even the potential beneficiaries of manpower reorganization—the mayors, and to a lesser extent the governors—showed less enthusiasm for the niceties of procedures than for the dollars they hoped to gain.

Thus the advocates of reorganization found themselves confronted not only with deep conflicts over the direction reform should take; but they also were confronted by the relative political disadvantages of procedural, as opposed to substantive, innovations.

7

Manpower and Functional Federalism: The Future View

As the 1970s dawned, a significant number of citizens were questioning the efficacy of governmental efforts to alleviate unemployment and underemployment. Scores of remedial manpower programs were in operation, millions of citizens had received assistance in one form or another, and several billion dollars were spent annually to help people prepare for, and adjust to, the world of work. Yet the problems of ill-prepared or ill-adjusted workers remained; and tales of waste, inefficiency, and failure were frequently dredged up. After all, what federal funds do not inevitably find their way into activities which *some* citizens find objectionable? The frustration was all the more intense because citizens no longer believed that workers should be condemned to suffer from impersonal or immutable economic forces. The problem could surely be solved; the citizens themselves had paid for solving them. Why then was no relief in sight?

Unquestionably, such complaints were based in large part upon faulty assumptions. The government's manpower efforts have, after all, given training, jobs, income, and services to millions of people who would have otherwise lacked those commodities. Convincing data on the impact of such data are invariably rarer than sensational accounts of failures. Moreover, despite phenomenal

96

increases in such programs (tenfold in the 1960s), such programs typically fall short of ideal funding—if for no other reason than that each program must compete with the others for the federal dollar. Although citizens and their elected officials expect action to reduce unemployment, they are too rarely willing to grant either the money or the time that is required to attain the solutions.

The notion that manpower policies can "solve unemployment" is in itself misleadingly simplistic. Governmental intervention is supplementary and interstitial, in relation to the basic operations of the labor market and the individual decisions of employers, workers, buyers, and other economic or political actors. The social and economic phenomenon of the unprepared or jobless worker is probably too complex a problem to be "solved" simply or single-handedly by even the most intelligent and concerted public action. A more realistic goal would be the amelioration of the problem and prevention of some of its more damaging consequences.

FUNCTIONAL FEDERALISM IN MANPOWER

At least as an intellectual proposition, few knowledgeable observers would today dispute the need for considerable consolidation and coordination of governmental programs. No one knows exactly how many governmental services there are; but the latest *Catalogue of Federal Domestic Assistance* lists more than a thousand separate programs, accounting for almost $40 billion annually and a fourth of all state and local revenues.

These programs have been erected more or less one at a time over the years, as each new pressing need was identified and a federal remedy devised. There is nothing very surprising about this phenomenon. Public perception of manpower problems undoubtedly proceeds in relatively limited, concrete terms. The citizen knows that he, or one of his family is out of work or that jobs are scarce, or that "business is bad." Liberal habits having been deeply ingrained, he expects his representatives in government to "do something about it." Elected officials, in turn, look around for a specific solution in the form of a policy, a program, or a piece of legislation. The structure of Congress reinforces this tendency to deal in specifics: the congressional committees handling manpower legislation have little expertise, much less authority, to delve into such matters as agricultural subsidies, selective service, or the size of the defense budget—all of which exert a more basic impact upon labor markets than do the training programs they authorize. As we have seen, a thorough and sophisticated legislative review of the full panoply of manpower programs is not a frequent occurrence.

Thus government has responded to employment problems in an incremental fashion. Vocational education was designed as a general aid to the nation's labor force; the employment service, a product of Depression joblessness, functioned traditionally as a labor exchange. The newer programs of the 1960s had a variety of objectives. MDTA was originally fashioned as an antidote to structural unemployment, but subsequent amendments directed it more to the needs of disadvantaged workers. The antipoverty programs also aimed at the disadvantaged. By the end of the 1960s, the federal government had assembled a full range of manpower services; but these programs added up to something less than a coherent whole.

This fragmented response to manpower problems is reinforced as governmental agencies are created or designated to administer the program or policy. The agencies soon developed their "missions"—goals, traditions, and standards of performance. The more dedicated and effective the agency's personnel, in fact, the more quickly they became imbued with the notion that their tasks were indispensable, that those tasks should be continued and even enlarged, and that the agency should have relatively unfettered authority to perform them. Rival agencies were viewed with suspicion. Relationships with congressional committees on the one hand, and with localized clienteles on the other, were cultivated to protect the agencies and their programs from incursions. Clientele organizations, if they did not exist previously, quickly sprang up to express and defend the interests of those who benefited from the programs. We have alluded to the role which these agency rivalries played in the struggle over manpower reform. The overall trends of the late 1960s were in the direction of consolidating the authority of the Manpower Administration's top management over manpower programs in the Labor Department; and in turn, that department's growing preeminence over OEO, HEW, and other agencies. However, the tensions created by these developments were manifest in the political events we have described.

In its role as initiator of manpower programs, the federal government disseminates funds and policies through state and local entities (Job Corps is an exception), creating in the process internally integrated functional subsystems. This is the phenomenon known as "functional federalism."[1] The system of categorical grants has fundamentally altered the traditional "layer-cake" view of federalism (federal; state; local), leaving instead in its place a series of vertical programmatic compartments. In each of these compartments, administrators at all governmental levels develop professional ties, common values, and shared viewpoints surrounding their tasks. While these bureaucrats often quarrel among themselves, they have very little in common with elected officials—legislative or executive—at their own governmental level. Having erected a wall of professionalism around their activities, these bureaucrats resist the intrusion of "outsiders." The employment service, as we have noted, is a stellar example of functional federalism in operation.

Broadly speaking, manpower programs operate under either federal-state or federal-local administrative delivery systems. In other words, the relevant federal agency delegates operating responsibility to state agencies, or to local prime sponsors under direct contracts. In the former category are most of the older programs, such as aid to vocational education and the employment

[1] The phrase comes from Selma J. Mushkin and John F. Cotton (with Gabrielle C. Lup), *Functional Federalism: Grants-in-Aid and PPB Systems* (Washington: The George Washington University State-Local Finances Project, November 1968). See also U.S. Senate, Committee on Government Operations, Subcommittee on Intergovernmental Relations, *The Federal System as Seen by Federal Aid Officials*, Staff Study, 89th Cong., 1st sess., December 15, 1965, pp. 93–102.

service. The latter category includes many of the newer programs of the 1960s, implemented as outgrowths of MDTA or EOA. Administrative patterns vary from area to area, but certain overall tendencies are clear.

At the state level, the most salient features in the administration of manpower services are the proliferation of agencies and the weakness of governors in coordinating the programs. From their survey of the fifty states, Howard Hallman and his associates concluded:

> In no state are all manpower programs under the jurisdiction of a single agency. Instead there is vast fragmentation of manpower agencies within state government, each in charge of one segment, but nobody responsible for orchestrating and coordinating the administration of a comprehensive state manpower program.[2]

Older manpower agencies—the employment service; public welfare; apprenticeship; and vocational education and rehabilitation—were organized to be largely autonomous and out of the reach of partisan politics. The programs of the 1960s, while seldom resulting in new administrative agencies, reinforced the dispersion of state level responsibilities. Funds either went directly to the established state agencies, or bypassed the states altogether in favor of local sponsors. Thus MDTA institutional funds were shared by state employment services and vocational education agencies; money for on-the-job training went to a variety of bodies—state and local agencies, national associations, and even private employers. The Work Incentive Program (WIN) gave the referral role to welfare agencies and the training role to the employment service.

In a few states, new human resource agencies have been established with broad powers and closer ties to the governor. But these remain the exception rather than the rule.

Local agencies are the ultimate deliverers of the bulk of education, training, and welfare services. Local governments have en-

[2] Howard W. Hallman, Everett Crawford, and Alden F. Briscoe, *State Manpower Organization* (Washington, D.C.: Center for Governmental Studies, July 1970), p. 16.

countered difficulty in planning and coordinating these services, however. Jurisdictional lines rarely encompass an entire labor market: the Philadelphia labor market, for example, boasts nearly a thousand governments of different types, including 8 counties, 140 municipalities, 199 townships, 331 school districts, and 286 special districts.[3] Thus local government units are often far too small in area or population to sustain effective services, much less coordinate a variety of area-wide functions. Like the states, municipal governments display many administrative defects: outdated civil service procedures and criteria; fragmented planning; coordination and communication among agencies; poor information and monitoring systems; limited accountability, especially to ghetto residents; and tendency toward a "crisis" style of management. Underlying these structures is an essentially pluralistic, fragmented structure of local politics.[4]

In this light the term "city hall" tends to denote a place but not an administrative or political entity. As one report put it, "In some local areas, the complex of agencies and programs resembled numerous games being played at the same time on the same field with some players participating simultaneously in different games."[5] As local officials began to sense the possibilities for involvement, especially through the manpower programs of the 1960s, their interest in controlling them was whetted—a factor of importance in the evolution of the 1970 manpower legislation.

The organization and delivery of manpower services is widely conceded to need general overhaul. Operated by a variety of agencies at federal, state, and local levels, the single purpose programs are aimed at diverse clienteles and needs, and vary in

[3] Howard Hallman, Everett Crawford, and Alden F. Briscoe, *Metropolitan Manpower Organization* (Washington, D.C.: Center for Governmental Studies, July 1970), p. 22.

[4] David Rogers, *Interest Groups, Coalitions, and Antipoverty Programs in Inner-Cities* (Ithaca: New York State School of Industrial and Labor Relations, Cornell University, April 1969).

[5] Committee for Economic Development, *Training and Jobs for the Urban Poor* (New York: Committee for Economic Development, July 1970), p. 39.

eligibility standards, benefit levels, application procedures, and methods of delivery. Some 10,000 separate contracts are in force at any given time between federal officials and public or private delivery agencies. Because services are fragmented and frequently uncoordinated, clients often cannot find the help they need.

Most commentators agree that the goal should be a one-stop, individualized service. A person in need of manpower services should be able to receive help, or at least referral to others who can help him, through a single, easily accessible local agency with the capability to assess his needs and then purchase or provide the prescribed services. The localized agency should be linked to systematic information about manpower needs and supplies for an entire labor market area, or even beyond. To plan the needed mixture of services for a locale, a centralized but representative decisionmaking process should be operative.

Administrative confusion, however, is not the only consequence of functional federalism. If it were, managerial tinkering might serve to achieve the desired efficiency. A key defect of functional federalism is political rather than administrative: namely, that these functional arenas are not *representative*—or rather, that they insulate the technicians who implement programs from the needs and demands of clients, potential clients, or even voters in the community. In other words, the full play of political forces at any given level in the system is rarely brought to bear on the functional fiefdoms. One manifestation of this defect is the relative lack of control which central-government officials—executives and legislators—exercise over the policy direction of the programs.

At the federal level, Congress establishes overall priorities but devotes only marginal attention to administrative oversight. And with rare exceptions, presidents have been unwilling or unable to exercise effective control over agencies and programs. At the state and local level, there has been almost no accountability because elected officials have for the most part been inactive bystanders in manpower efforts. Federal bureaucrats have been relied upon to monitor projects, however imperfectly. Those decisions which are left to local agencies tend to have been technical and usually made by the employment service or the state vocational education department. Such agencies are typically free from direct political control, operating normally as self-sustaining bureaucracies. Because their budgets and personnel are normally not dependent upon the state decisionmaking process, these agencies are "irresponsible"—in the precise political meaning of the term.

Political accountability was broadened somewhat in the mid-1960s with the antipoverty program's effort to foster "maximum feasible participation" by the disadvantaged. This was nothing less than a bid to open up the functional closure that had historically marked manpower and other welfare programs. The voice of the poor was heard throughout the land, sometimes with invigorating and provocative effects. But the experiment generated strong counterpressures, as functional bureaucracies launched concerted attempts to regain or retain control over their programs. By the end of the 1960s, the community action agencies—though alive and well—posed only a minor threat to established bureaucratic agencies.

In short, the public has very little chance to participate in setting the direction of manpower programs. The problem is, therefore, not how to get politics *out of* manpower programs, but how to inject more of the healthy combat of politics *into* them.

If reform is widely conceded to be necessary, efforts in that direction are, as we have seen, fraught with difficulty. Invariably, the interests of functional federalism insist that federal funds be earmarked for the various purposes they champion, and that their functions be given autonomy from those of rival bureaucracies. Thus the structure of functional federalism has proved to be frustratingly resistant to change; and there have been few successful instances where major revisions have been pushed through.

One example is sufficient to illustrate the typical pattern. In 1955 the Commission on Intergovernmental Relations (the Kestnbaum Commission), after more than two years of labor, settled on one federal program which it thought could be turned back completely to the states. This program was vocational education. The commission concluded that federal aid to vocational education, in existence since 1917, had outlived its usefulness, and that in any event the federal contribution was not essential. Although the commission made its recommendations to Congress as far back as 1955, at last report vocational education was alive and thriving in Washington, with federal aid multiplying more than tenfold in the meantime.

In defending their piece of the action, vocational educators argued that their program would suffer because the states or localities might not vote the money. Functional interests can hardly be expected to react otherwise: why should they wish to exchange the admitted problems of grants-in-aid for the unknown terrors of uncategorized revenue-sharing?

These interests therefore wrap themselves in the public interest and argue that it is to the nation's advantage that their programs be assured continued funding. They also contend that grants-in-aid permit the federal government to redistribute money more easily to needy areas (within a single state as well as among states); and that "no strings" aid will offer no assurance that national standards (such as civil rights or fair labor practices) will be adhered to.

Testifying in favor of revenue-sharing in 1969, Chairman Robert E. Merriam of the Advisory Commission on Intergovernmental Relations explained why functional federalism is so tenacious:

. . . legislative and executive bodies at all levels are organized along particular functional lines and tend, therefore, to focus on specific programs rather than on the strength and vitality of the government entities. Indeed, if experience has any lessons for us it is that the particular interests always tend to overrun the general. Short-run demand to beef up a particular program tends to override the long-range need to strengthen the instrumentalities for delivering program results, in this case state and local governments.[6]

The message is clear: adequate groundwork, both conceptual and practical, must be laid down before the particularism and confusion of functional federalism can be overcome.

[6] U.S. Senate, Committee on Government Operations, Subcommittee on Intergovernmental Relations, *Intergovernmental Revenue Act of 1969 and Related Legislation*, 91st Cong., 2nd sess., 1970, p. 300.

CONCEPTUAL GROUNDWORK: CLARIFYING THE GOALS

Unfortunately, the defenders and detractors of traditional federal programs tend to talk past one another, becoming conscientious objectors in each one's vision of what the future should be. To the administrators of federal grant programs and their cheerleaders both in and out of government, the reformers are simply visionaries who do not understand how politics works. The reformers, on the other hand, regard their opponents as nefarious protectors of special interests.

What is needed is a brand of pragmatic idealism. The political strength of functional federalism suggests that all-out warfare on those institutions would prove unfruitful. Compromises will have to be struck to gain adoption of reorganization plans. Mechanisms will have to be set in motion to accomplish the desired changes over a substantial period of time. But first, precision of reform goals would be helpful.

What, first of all, is meant by "decategorizing" programs? Surely it does not mean a truly wholistic approach to the manpower needs of the economy, for, however desirable this might be, no one has proposed this radical course of action. Considering the interconnectedness of all public policy—everything is related to everything else—a truly integrated manpower policy would stagger the imagination, since it would of necessity embrace almost every conceivable public agency and virtually every causative factor in the society. We cannot escape the fact that manpower needs depend upon a whole series of decisions, both private and public in locus, which shape both the structure and utilization of the labor market. In dealing with such complexity, limited categories of objectives and services are probably inevitable. Politically, they provide levers for people to grasp to influence and alter the order of public priorities. Categories are ways of giving emphasis, of changing one's mind without unraveling the entire fabric of policy. "We want to separate the wheat from the chaff and give senators an opportunity to deal with these matters individually," one senator remarked in regard to the legislative appropriations process.[7] The senator's remarks are indicative of the way in which political actors, and other people as well, utilize categories in bringing a semblance of order to a complex environment.

Actually, decategorization is a symbol of the *direction* of change being advocated. What is usually meant is merely that services should be administratively drawn together at the point where the potential client walks in the door asking for help. Equally important, programs should be placed side by side at the planning stage, where decisions can be reached as to the appropriate mixture of services within a given geographical area. To achieve these goals, rigid categorical funding practices should be eliminated or greatly curtailed, so that the priorities among categories can be adjusted more flexibly as needs or conditions dictate.

By the same token, the goal of decentralization must be refined. Indeed, it is questionable whether there are any *inherent* advantages of decentralization. Of course, everyone concedes that services should be conveniently available to potential clients. Perhaps this will mean more neighborhood centers where the clients live and work; perhaps not. But this is quite different from the question of where the planning and administrative locus of programs should lie.

For one thing, public services vary greatly in the amount of "spillover" which they possess—that is, the degree to which people outside of a given geographical area benefit indirectly from services rendered within that area.[8] Some badly needed services would simply not be undertaken if they depended upon the support of those in a given geographic area. Others, such as research and demonstration, can only be pursued efficiently on a nationwide basis.

It has yet to be demonstrated, for example, that local government is more efficient, more effective, or even "closer to the peo-

---

[7] Senator Norris Cotton (R-N.H.), on the Labor-HEW appropriations bill, *Congressional Record*, daily ed., November 20, 1970, p. S18605.

[8] See Dick Netzer, *State-Local Finance and Intergovernmental Fiscal Relations* (Washington, D.C.: The Brookings Institution, 1969).

ple" than alternative units of government. It is sometimes argued, or at least assumed, that the smaller the unit of government, the closer it is to the people and the more representative of their interests. This "doctrinal approach to decentralization," as James Fesler has termed it, tends to merge, and even confuse, decentralization and democracy.[9] In point of fact, however, the notion of "grass-roots democracy" is largely a myth.

The question of the comparative representativeness of political systems is one which, despite its obvious importance, has been given less attention by students than it certainly deserves. At minimum, however, it seems reasonable to recall the caveats implied by Fesler: first, that local governments' manpower decision-making processes assume many forms; and second, that no level of government boasts a "distinctive impulse" toward democracy. Indeed, decentralization can take place in the absence of local democracy.[10]

Insofar as we are in a position to generalize about the relative character of local and national manpower decisionmaking, the most plausible line of reason seems to favor the latter. That is, the larger a political arena, the more likely it is to be responsive to its full constituency, if by responsiveness is meant the ability to take into account a wide variety of political needs and demands. The reason, so the argument goes, lies simply in the fact that smaller political systems such as those of towns, villages, or counties, are more likely to embrace relatively homogeneous populations, and to be dominated by small locally based elites.[11] Minorities, of whatever type, are apt to be small and politically impotent. However imperfect in other respects, the large and heterogeneous constituencies seem to have responded with greater alacrity and sensitivity to the rights and needs of minority groups.

[9] James W. Fesler, "Approaches to the Understanding of Decentralization," in Duane Lockard (ed.), *Governing the States and Localities: Selected Readings* (New York: Macmillan, 1969), p. 38.

[10] Ibid.

[11] For a detailed exposition of this argument, see Grant McConnell, *Private Government and American Democracy* (New York: Alfred A. Knopf, 1966), esp. chap. 10.

MANPOWER AND FUNCTIONAL FEDERALISM

It is therefore no accident that in an affluent and middle-class society the national political apparatus responded initially to the problems of poverty, unemployment, and inadequate income.

There is no proof, moreover, that the average citizen identifies more strongly with government which is close to him than he does with government that is far away. Alienation from public institutions can, it is true, be fairly widespread, as in the late 1960s and early 1970s. But it is probably equally true that this alienation, when it occurs, strikes most harshly at local and state governments. The average citizen learns first about the actors of the national political system—the president, the Congress, and national political figures—and this identification is reinforced throughout his life by the enormous attention which the media give to national as opposed to state or local political life. Thus the average citizen knows more about national political and governmental institutions, exhibits more interest in them, feels they impinge more directly on his daily life, and expresses more confidence in their performance. As a result, the citizen is more apt to participate in national politics—a factor which further jeopardizes the representativeness of local institutions. Summarizing the findings, Thomas R. Dye has noted that "voter turnout in local elections is substantially lower than in state or national elections"—a phenomenon he describes as "another conservative influence on local government."[12]

One may applaud or condemn the underlying reasons for these phenomena; but their existence cannot reasonably be denied. Our brief discussion should be sufficient to establish that governmental responsiveness is not to be equated with geographic closeness. Moreover, it should now be apparent why conservative interests tend to support decentralization while liberals are suspicious of it. Certainly abstract principles are far from the only motivations of conventional positions on the matter.

Finally, the principle of decentralization begs the critical question: decentralization *to whom*? To the average person in need of

[12] Thomas R. Dye, *Politics of the States and Communities* (Englewood Cliffs, N.J.: Prentice-Hall, 1969), p. 224.

108

manpower services, the issue is not solely the locus of manpower decisions, but also whether the decisions are subject to a free exchange of political forces—whether, in a word, the decision is responsive to public needs or simply the product of an autonomous administrative structure. To be more specific, dumping manpower policy decisions into the hands of state or local officials would accomplish nothing if those officials were unprepared for them and simply turned them over to the local counterparts of the same functional subsystems which have been implementing manpower programs from the beginning—for example, local employment services or school districts. And there is every reason to believe that a decentralization effectuated too rapidly or with too little regard for the ultimate locus and character of manpower decision-making would lead to just such a result. For the foreseeable future, perhaps no more than a handful of states or metropolitan areas are prepared immediately to take over the reins of manpower decision-making in a way which would be more politically representative and administratively coherent than is presently the case.

The central question is thus not which *level* of government will manage these programs; but *who* will have access to the decision process. Shifting burdens from one agency to another, or even from Washington to the state capitals or city halls, has very little to do with this dilemma.

In short, the theory behind some of the proposed reforms is a faulty view of the federal system. This is the school child's notion that federal government is like the three-layer cake—federal, state, and local. Upon occasion President Nixon evidenced this theory of federalism by his contention that his goal was "to reverse the flow of power and resources from the states and communities to Washington, and start power and resources flowing back. . . ." Continuing the layer cake analogy, the president's goal is to give each governmental layer its proper weight and consistency.

The thrust of our argument is that our federal system does not now operate this way, if indeed it ever did. The functional bureaucracies, or "subgovernments," that have been created by activist government span all three levels of government, constituting functional or professional bureaucracies. It is as if the layer cake had been turned over on its side, leaving a series of vertical compartments rather than horizontal layers. Perhaps former North Carolina Governor Terry Sanford hit upon a more apt analogy when he likened the resultant federal system to a picket fence. Federal categorical grant-in-aid systems—"lines of authority, the concerns and interests, the flow of money, and the direction of programs"— are the pickets, the most visible portion of the fence. Federal, state, and local general governments are like the connecting cross slat which "does little to support anything. It holds the pickets in line, it does not bring them together."[13] Any attempts at reforming governmental services must come to grips with this fact of political life—which both causes the crisis in public services and frustrates its resolution. Can anything be done?

PRACTICAL GROUNDWORK: GUIDED DECENTRALIZATION

If the present system for dispensing manpower services has taken years to develop, a more effective system is not likely to spring forth overnight. It should be remembered that, in spite of its myriad defects, the present system of discrete and uncoordinated programs does a fairly commendable job of matching services and clients—given all of the institutional shortcomings and funding limitations. Effective reform will have to build on established patterns and shift them through judicious manipulation of structures and incentives.

That is to say, quick and easy solutions are illusory. As in most things, ideological flourishes are no substitute for careful planning and follow-through. For example, if "no-strings" manpower dollars were suddenly to be thrust upon unprepared local officials, the reaction of the majority would be to throw up their hands in dismay and turn the money over to the experts who have been running the federally funded programs since their origins. This could only have the effect of setting in concrete the very pattern which reformers

[13] Terry Sanford, *Storm over the States* (New York: McGraw-Hill, 1967), p. 80.

wish to modify: the growth of special functional units at the expense of a broadly representative decisionmaking system.

We wish to create a planning and delivery system that is coherent and representative; yet we cannot mandate the establishment of such a system. What can be done, however, is to set forth conditions that are likely to induce the results we have in mind, working through natural processes. Such a strategy was utilized in the Labor Department's CAMPS programs at the state and municipal levels. A planning function was delegated to a group whose structure was specified, and natural interactional processes were allowed to develop from that point. Officials developed the habit of working in concert (even if there was little in concrete terms for the CAMPS committees to do); and what was more important, there evolved in the CAMPS staffs a centrally-placed cadre of informed, experienced manpower generalists. Having developed expertise, they were understandably impatient to the paucity of decisions they were asked to make.

Sooner or later, agencies like these must be entrusted with decisions that count. This certainly means that allocation of funds among various services must be decentralized to them, perhaps in a phased arrangement. Budgetmaking is probably the single most compelling device for planning and choosing among priorities; certainly planning without budgetary power is an academic exercise. Local, area-wide, or state-wide planners must hold the budgetary reins firmly if they are to compel coordination among delivery agencies and make rational, flexible responses to changing demands. Federal agents—presumably officials in the Manpower Administration—should make money available on the basis of comprehensive service plans submitted by local prime sponsors; and these plans should also provide the basis for evaluation. Not only federal officials, but congressmen and senators as well, should be tolerant of mistakes made in the cause of local initiative.

The actual prime sponsor will vary with the situation. In some cases it will be a state manpower agency. It is clear, however, that the larger urban areas will insist upon, and receive, authority to control their own area-wide prime sponsors. In a majority of cases

111

the prime sponsorship will fall to an agency of the general government; but in no sense should this be thought the exclusive pattern. The more important point is that the prime sponsor be in a position to coordinate existing manpower service systems; and that its decision processes be open to all the relevant interests, including recipients of services.

In approving the *content* of manpower service plans, federal agents should assume a posture of encouragement with restraint. As one astute observer has phrased it,

> The essential role [of the Department of Labor] is to provide leadership for the national manpower system. This requires the Department to be affirmative, more concerned with what can be done than with what ought not be done.[14]

Guidelines should be merely that, and not specifications or directions. Research, experimentation, and technical assistance are eminently the province of the federal agency.

If federal policymakers ought to be permissive in tolerating local initiative in program content and mix, they should be aggressive in assuring that *procedures* for developing and implementing local manpower plans are acceptable. Here is the point at which a strings-attached aid program can have the most far-reaching payoff. Whatever the prime sponsor, the secretary of labor should insist that it be adequately staffed; that it follow accepted procedures; and that it be accountable to the citizens within its operating area. Federal officials should stand ready to contribute technical assistance and grants to upgrade staffing, infuse better management techniques, and ensure public responsiveness. Moreover, they should be in a position to require that comprehensive manpower plans be designed and implemented with the "maximum feasible participation" of area residents and the groups served.

No more than a handful of state and local political systems now possess the strength they would need to pull manpower dollars together and make them accountable to the local political

---

[14] Howard W. Hallman, *Achieving Full Employment: The Role of Manpower Programs* (Washington, D.C.: Center for Governmental Studies, 1972), p. 28.

process. Efforts to build up the planning and supervisory capabilities of central governments are underway but by no means completed. What eventually will be needed will be new constitutional powers for the chief executive, new professional standards for elected bodies such as legislatures and the city councils, new expertise for local administrators, and a strengthened voice for community groups (including the disadvantaged)—in short, a more representative and authoritative system for policymaking.

The combination strategy I am putting forward thus consists of (a) decentralized lump-sum funding; (b) programmatic flexibility; and (c) procedural rigor. It is contended that such a strategy has the best chance of encouraging and building permanent manpower decisionmaking systems at the service-area level. To be sure, the solution will require more restraint than federal bureaucrats and legislators are in the habit of demonstrating toward local grantees. But in one key respect the federal role would be more purposeful and more aggressive than in the past: namely, the federal grantor should exercise care in selecting local prime sponsors (and shifting them, if necessary); should be ready to provide funds and advice to prime sponsors to make their operations and staffs more professional; and should *require* that the comprehensive manpower plans be arrived at through a politically open, responsive process. The objective is not so much a specified set of services, as a set of viable decisionmaking systems at the state, area, and local levels.

The outward form of such a reorganization would undoubtedly very closely resemble a streamlined bloc-grant arrangement that would permit selective decentralization of nationally funded services at the same time that the desired political and administrative reforms were being built at the subnational level. The features of a streamlined grant system are fairly simple in the abstract, though they will certainly reflect infinite variety in application. They are by no means to be considered the end result of reform; but they are a reasonable approximation which will lay the groundwork for the eventual desired results. Such a streamlined grant system would include the following elements:

A. In the first instance, state and local general governments would be responsible for pulling together plans and arriving at the "mix" of programs that is most appropriate for them.

B. The relevant federal agency (preferably acting through its regional offices) would then review the program according to the broadest possible criteria, to see that certain basic federal standards are met.

C. The state and local general governments would provide the services to coordinate them—usually relying upon existing local institutions to provide the actual services.

D. The federal government (again working primarily through regional offices) would evaluate the services that have been provided not only to assure compliance with federal standards, but also in light of the objectives which the state or local entities had specified. In other words, the state and local governments would be judged in large measure against the standard they had set for themselves.

E. Portions of the grant should be set aside for central governments to develop planning and coordinating capabilities.

F. Standards should be set for the "maximum feasible participation" of relevant individuals and groups—perhaps through local and state manpower planning councils of the kind included in the Employment and Manpower Act (S.3867).

G. The residual functions of the federal agency would include: sponsoring research, undertaking experimental and demonstration projects, giving technical assistance, aiding interstate communication, and in a few cases providing the services directly if the state or locality is unwilling or unable to do so.

Gradual devolution of such streamlined grant programs to the states and localities could be built into such programs. In other words, as local administrative mechanisms and administrative processes were strengthened (through meeting federally set standards and applying grant monies), the proportion of monies decentralized to the state and local prime sponsors could be increased over a period of years. The point to be made is that the turnover should not be sudden, or in any event in advance of the evolving capacities of the local or state prime sponsors.

A system of streamlined bloc-grant programs would lay the groundwork for a truly healthy decentralized federal system by paring down the Washington establishment while at the same time revitalizing state and local general governments for the enlarged role they would play. Some governors and mayors could perhaps handle the transition easily, but for most such a capability is a decade or even generation away. Functional federalism was not built in a day; and it will take as much to transform the accumulated institutional and political forces that have grown up in the last fifty years or so. Politics, as Max Weber once wrote, is a tedious hewing at stubborn timber; and so political and administrative reform will require years of careful and unglamorous institutional handiwork.

70921